"Blessed Grievin [...] [...] *one who has bee* [...] [...] *mense awareness* [...] [...] *ity and invites us into our own.* [...] There are [...] which people decide to write and there are books written out of necessity. Blessing Life's Losses *is the latter. Joan had to write it, but we are the beneficiaries."*

—Richard Rohr, OFM,
Center for Action and Contemplation,
Albuquerque, New Mexico

"Healing the wounds of human loss requires both an intellectual and an emotional grieving process. Blessing Life's Losses *provides an excellent process for both, together with the added dimension of spiritual reflection. When human grief can be experienced as a step toward personal growth and spiritual health, the human spirit can be transformed."*

—Helen Flaherty, SC
Past president of the National Leadership
Conference of Women Religious

"In this wonderful book Joan Guntzelman provides the reader with the opportunity to deal with life's losses in a manner leading not only to resolution but also to personal and spiritual growth. Her gentle but powerful words offer an authentic, practical, and highly personalized pathway through the grieving process. I will enthusiastically recommend this unique work to my patients, students, and peers."

—Gregory Franchini, MD, Director
Medical Student Education in Psychiatry,
University of New Mexico,
Albuquerque, New Mexico

Blessing
Life's Losses

Letting Go and Moving On

Joan Guntzelman

Liguori
LIGUORI, MISSOURI

Imprimi Potest:
Richard Thibodeau, C.Ss.R.
Provincial, Denver Province
The Redemptorists

Published by Liguori Publications
Liguori, Missouri
www.liguori.org

Library of Congress Cataloging-in-Publication Data

Guntzelman, Joan, 1937–
    [Blessed grieving]
    Blessing life's losses : letting go and moving on / Joan Guntzelman.
        p. cm.
    Originally published: Blessed grieving. Winona, Minn. : St. Mary's Press, Christian Brothers Publications, © 1994.
    ISBN 0-7648-1152-5
    1. Loss (Psychology)—Religious aspects—Catholic Church. 2. Grief— Religious aspects—Catholic Church. I. Title.

BX2373.S5G857 2004
242'.4—dc22   2003069493

The acknowledgments continue on page 129.

Printed in the United States of America
08 07 06 05 04   5 4 3 2 1
Revised edition 2004

Contents

Introduction

"Blessed Are Those Who Grieve..."

Several years ago, ferocious winds felled groves of lodge-pole pines in one of the most beautiful sections of Grand Teton National Park. The Forest Service erected a sign explaining: "In order for a living forest to continue to exist, we depend on three things: blowdowns, like the one that occurred here, when wind speed reaches such a degree that old, weak, unhealthy, and even some strong and healthy trees are uprooted or felled; a type of beetle infestation that destroys trees; and forest fires." That sign captured the pattern of our universe—in order for life to continue, we *need* loss and death.

Losses are constant. We do not live long in this world without loss and its attendant hurt. Of course, we are also continually surrounded by beauty and goodness, if we have the eyes to see them. However, unless we have a painful loss or an ecstatic moment, we tend to give little or no thought to the pattern of the universe: loss and growth, death and life. Loss and growth are partners. Death and life are two sides of the same coin. As Job exclaimed: "Shall we receive the good at the hand of God, and not receive the bad?" (2:10, NRSV).

Not all loss is of the same magnitude or kind. It comes in an infinite variety of ways—sometimes it is barely noticeable; at other times, it is overwhelmingly apparent. All loss can be the groundwork for new life and growth. Nature supplies abundant examples. For instance, the loss of the limy greenness of the aspen leaf makes way for the shimmering gold of a brilliant fall. The caterpillar that goes into the darkness and silence of the cocoon must stop being a caterpillar in order to become a brilliant butterfly. Our bodies are steadily repairing and re-creating themselves. New cells constantly replace dead cells. Within each human body, the processes of death and life, loss and growth, continue.

Stages of Human Loss and Growth

Loss and growth proceed in each season of life. Our first loss comes when we pass out of the protecting womb and into the world. When we venture into the tumult of school, the simplicity of a world of family gives way to lessons, performance, and getting along with other people.

Growth in the form of experience and learning propels us out of childhood and into adolescence. People begin to expect us to act grown up. With the loss of our child body, most of us also lose our child innocence. We discover that we are capable of evil, and we vacillate between childhood dependence and the adult demand for independence. We strike out into a broader world and expand our intellectual and emotional horizons.

In young adulthood the process continues. Amid the joy of finding intimacy and establishing a career, the shadow of loss lurks. One young woman, who was about to be married, opted for counseling with me because she was feeling sad and did not understand why. She was delighted about marrying a man she dearly loved, but she overlooked the losses that can come with marriage: losses of independence, privacy, her own home, and coming and going as she pleased. Once she recognized those gifts, she willingly opted to give them up for the sake of marriage. The losses, however, asked for her awareness and some expression of grief at their passing.

At midlife, we become increasingly tuned in to how the losses have accumulated. Although we can exercise and develop endurance, we just cannot compete with younger people in physical activity. Childbearing years come to an end. Jobs wished for or worked toward begin to fall into the hands of younger people. Children grow up and leave home. Other dreams fade into anguished memory.

On the other hand, people at midlife often see the fruits of their labor. Careers have reached a high point. Valuable wisdom has been accumulated, especially by those who have made an inner journey and established a deeper relationship with family, friends, themselves, and God.

As we continue to age, we may be overwhelmed by the magnitude of our losses. Physical losses are compounded. "I want to do so much, but my body just won't let me" is a common frustration. Our eyes begin to fail. No one seems to speak distinctly. Friends, family members, and even a spouse may have died, leaving us with tremendous grief.

Yet being older gives us a broader perspective on problems. We may have the leisure time to do things we have always wanted to do. We may appreciate God's small gifts more fully.

- ❖ Make a "loss history" of your life—identify all the things you have left behind and note how you have managed to move beyond them.
- ❖ Which losses of aging are or will be most difficult for you?

Our Losses Are *Our* Losses

Losses may look the same on the surface, but they are always unique to each individual. While two people may lose the same object, person, position, or dream, the experience is never the same.

When we grieve, we grieve the loss of what something meant to us, as well as the lost object itself. This may be why two persons with the same external loss suffer differently. Both Mary Ann and Joyce experienced the death of their husband. Joyce described her husband as her best friend and constant companion, one on whom she depended and whose company she enjoyed through nearly thirty years of marriage. Mary Ann, however, felt relieved after the loss of her abusive husband.

Our losses are unique because our perception of each loss is unique. As we connect with a variety of people, objects, ideas, wishes, values, images, and roles, we give them great power within us. We form our identity through these connections, and we invest them with meaning and symbolic importance.

When we lose any of these connections, we lose not only the thing itself but also what it represented for us and the meaning we invested in it. For example, a man whose personal identity is strongly connected with his job may grieve profoundly over the loss of that job. For a man who sees a job as merely the necessary means to earn money so he can involve himself in other pursuits, the loss of his job may be simply a nuisance. His sense of identity is untouched.

Frequently, we do not realize how much meaning we have invested in something until we lose it. I recall a patient who was excited about leaving her job in a big office to begin working for herself. She had dreamed of establishing her own business for years and methodically set about making her dream come true. She had no idea, however, how much she valued the companionship and daily interaction with her coworkers. She was unprepared for the sadness and loneliness that she felt when she was finally on her own.

Change always brings loss, even when the change is welcome. Many parents look forward to a child going off to college, but tears flow when they see their son or daughter in the rearview mirror. At home, the house seems empty and somehow sad.

Responses to Loss

Just as our losses are unique to each of us, so are our ways of coping with loss. As children, we imitated the way our parents grieved their losses. Over time, we learned certain coping mechanisms. Each time we use a particular method of coping, it becomes more deeply ingrained into a pattern of dealing with life. Finally we may believe that we do not have choices about our response to loss. Some of what we learned and what was rewarded in our behavior served us well. However, our parents, grandparents, and teachers, being imperfect people, sometimes taught and rewarded ways of behaving that later did not work well for us. One adult task is to examine what we learned, hold on to what is healthy, and discard what is not. Many unhealthy ways of coping with today's losses began in early messages like "Big boys don't cry" or "Don't be such a sissy."

Some ways of handling loss seem to be fairly common. We can profit by examining these prevalent reactions and considering how they play out in our own life.

Denial or disbelief. Most of us, in our initial confrontation with a loss, have trouble *believing* it to be true. We hear ourselves saying things like "I can't believe he'd really leave!" or "Oh, no! That can't be!" This kind of reaction gives us the time we need to adjust to the change. We sometimes choose to stay in such denial, thinking that as long as we hang on to disbelief, the loss won't be true.

Anger. Whenever we come up against our inability to control forces in our life, especially when we believe we need that control for our happiness and well-being, we often react with anger. We look for someone or something to blame for our pain or misfortune. Anger associated with a loss may be directed toward God or toward others who had a part in our loss—the supervisor who told us we didn't get the job, the doctor who announced a difficult diagnosis—or even someone not involved who seems untouched by our pain.

Guilt. Many times we conclude that we have brought about our own loss. Guilt can then sweep over us. The dog owner who never used a leash may feel deep guilt when the animal is killed by a car. The lonely elder who never had time for pleasantries and friendliness comes to realize that she designed her own loneliness. Guilt may ride heavily when we recognize our own role in our losses.

Sometimes we attribute guilt to ourselves even when our loss is simply part of the story of life. After learning that she had cancer, one woman told me, "I've always believed that you get out of life what you put into it. I thought I was putting good things into life, but I guess I wasn't or this wouldn't have happened to me." Even though loss happens to everyone, we have commonly been taught that everything that happens to us is somehow our fault, leaving us with guilt when something bad does happen.

Sadness. Whenever life takes away or asks us to let go of something that we have recognized as part of us, we can expect sadness.

When something is lost from our life, many other reactions and emotions may boil up: fear, rage, despair, confusion, loneliness. No magic formula or scientific scale tells us how much or how little of any reaction we can expect.

So we must be careful in judging the value of some-

xiv   *Introduction*

one else's losses, as well as their style of coping. A loss may appear of more or less value on the surface but may have different meanings in the heart of the person experiencing it.

- ❖ How have you been taught to deal with losses in your life?
- ❖ When you were a child, what did your parents or other significant people tell you about showing your emotions?
- ❖ What are the losses in your own life that you're still having trouble releasing?
- ❖ Are you willing to see the treasure your own life is, filled with opportunities for growth through the losses you've experienced?

Each Loss Is an Opportunity

Response to loss is a sign that life is happening through everything we experience. In our own history and experience of loss, we will find the makings of ourself. Indeed, our whole life is full of opportunities for growth, for wholeness, for holiness. When Jesus says, "For those who want to follow me, let them take up their cross every day and follow me" (adapted from Luke 9:23), we might hear him saying to each of us, "Take up the burden of your own life, with all its blessings and all its sorrows and losses and deaths. Take it up, don't minimize it, try to ignore it, or look elsewhere for holiness. The opportunities are all right there, in your very own life. Take them up, look at them, grieve over them, and give them to me. Let them go."

While we often cannot control the losses in our life, we have a lot to say about how we handle them. Though we feel like we have little control, every day we are choosing the ways we deal with loss.

Loss in Christian Living

Life resurrecting out of death forms the heart of Christian living. Jesus proclaimed, in both his words and his example, that unless we are willing to die, we will never live. He illustrated this point—the paschal mystery—with a common event in nature: "Unless a wheat grain falls into the earth and dies, it remains only a single grain; but if it dies it yields a rich harvest" (John 12:24, NJB). Any farmer or gardener knows that to have life, every seed must burst apart and let go of what it is, push its stem up into the sun and its roots down through the darkness.

Yet we always ask why we must suffer loss. And the answer always ends with mystery. When Job asked God why he had to lose everything—his land, his family, his health, and even his hope, God answered him with questions: "Where were you when I laid the foundation of the earth? / Tell me, if you have understanding. / Who determined its measurements—surely you know!" (Job 38:4–5, NRSV). Human beings, like all of creation, live and die.

God does not will suffering on us. That we know. Rather, Jesus says: "I came that they may have life, and have it abundantly" (John 10:10, NRSV). Indeed, this abundant life that God wishes for us was paradoxically manifested in the life of Jesus, "who, though he was in the form of God, / did not regard equality with God / as something to be exploited, / but…[was] born in human likeness…./ He humbled himself and became obedient to the point of death—/ even death on a cross" (Philippians 2:6–8, NRSV). Jesus lived a full life, but it did not spare him from suffering and death.

Fullness of life comes from doing God's will, which, in its broadest terms, means loving God and loving our neighbors as ourselves. Love brings not only joy, wonder, and life but also pain, mundane struggles, and death. But through the Resurrection of Jesus, death does not have the last word. Life triumphs. And always, the Spirit of God dwells with us to support and console us. Knowing that his departure would grieve his followers, Jesus promised: "God will send you another Advocate…the Spirit will be in you. I will not leave you orphaned; I am coming to you" (adapted from John 14:16–18). Even with their faith in this guarantee, the disciples mourned Jesus' death.

An eloquent description of the Christian response to suffering and grief came in an interview between Sister Thea Bowman and Patrice Tuohy. Sister Thea was a teacher, a singer, and a lecturer who spread the Good News to all people and tirelessly promoted pride in black culture. After interviewing Thea for television's *60 Minutes*, CBS correspondent Mike Wallace said, "I don't remember when I've been more moved, more enchanted by a person whom I've profiled" (Cepress, *Sister Thea Bowman: Shooting Star*). Sister Thea knew, after six years of living with cancer, that her life was almost at an end. In her interview with Tuohy, this is what Thea said about suffering and hope:

Tuohy: How do you make sense out of your pain and suffering?

Bowman: I don't make sense of it [suffering]. I try to make sense of life. I try to keep myself open to people and to laughter and to love and to have faith....I pray, "Oh Jesus, I surrender."...I console myself with the old Negro spiritual: "Sooner will be done the troubles of this world. I'm going home to live with God."

Tuohy: Is God really present in suffering?

Bowman: God is present in everything....In me and all that happens to me...everywhere. In the midst of suffering, I feel God's presence and cry out to God for help: "Lord, help me to hold on."

Tuohy: Why do people have to suffer? What possible good can come from it?

Bowman: I don't know. Why is there war? Why is there hunger?...Perhaps it's an incentive for struggling human beings to reach out to one another, to help one another, to love one another, to be blessed and strengthened and humanized in the process. Perhaps it's an incentive to see Christ in our world and to view the work of Christ and feel the suffering of Christ.

I remember the words of an old song: "We've come this far by faith, leaning on the Lord, trusting in his words. The Lord has never failed us yet. Oh, can't turn around because we've come this way by faith."

—*Tuohy, "Sister Thea Bowman:*
On the Road to Glory"

Jesus invites us to grow day by day through the dying and rising experiences of our lives. And the growth and rising happen best when we are conscious of and say yes to all sizes and sorts of losses and deaths.

How Do We Grow Through Losses?

In each of our experiences of loss, we choose to move toward life or death. Each option is always present. Moses offered that same choice to the Israelites when he said, "I set before you life or death...choose life..." (adapted from Deuteronomy 30:19). We often do not even know that we *have* choices to make.

Most of us tend to focus on the positive aspects of our life, secretly believing that loss is unnecessary, unfortunate, avoidable, unlucky, and an aberration. Insufficient attention has been directed toward the role loss plays in life.

No one teaches us that the only way new growth comes is through loss. No one tells us that loss is normal and natural. No one informs us that the only time change stops is after death. No one purposefully shows us how to cope with it. Six months after the death of his wife in childbirth, one young man cried out in anguish to his minister, "They taught us everything else in growing up—why didn't they teach us how to deal with things like this?"

As tragic, as untimely, as dreaded, and as feared as loss and death may be, none of us will ever be able to avoid them. But we can begin to acknowledge the losses in our own life and learn to live and grow through them. Choosing to grow and be born through small losses helps us to make that same choice in bigger losses. Life is the continuous process of giving birth to ourselves.

To grieve well involves our thoughts, our feelings, and our behavior. Healthy, growthful grieving typically includes three movements:

1. We begin grieving when we openly acknowledge what has been lost.
2. We express whatever feelings and emotions are called forth when we acknowledge the loss.
3. We choose to change the things we do that keep us tied to the lost person or object.

While these three aspects of grieving are described separately, in practice they usually intertwine. For instance, in the very act of acknowledging a loss, our emotions frequently surface and spill over. Changing a certain way of doing things because of a loss may intensify our awareness of the loss and arouse more emotion. In any case, as we make our way through these three phases, we are usually on the road to renewing our life.

❖ Call to mind any losses in your own life that you have never thought about before. Identify at least one loss that was necessary before something else that you wanted could come into your life.

❖ Ponder the pattern of dying and living again that underlies your own experience.

Acknowledging What Has Been Lost

The first movement in healthy grieving takes place when we willingly and openly acknowledge what has been lost. We begin making our way through our losses by bringing them to our awareness. Often, everything in us wants to deny that a loss is real, wants to believe that nothing has changed. We must eventually be able to acknowledge the reality of what was lost, however, because until we recognize it, we will not be able to grieve its loss.

When we fail to acknowledge a loss, or refuse to grieve over it, the sense of loss does not simply disappear. Important aspects of our life that are ignored or minimized tend to escalate and struggle for our attention. We may have an uneasy feeling that something is bothering us, and find that it begins to affect us and gain power within us.

Taking inventory of our own history of losses may start us on a powerful journey toward self-awareness and understanding. We may get in touch with long-buried pain and sadness that we have tried to convince ourselves is unimportant. We may find ourself clinging to pain and sadness in a refusal to let go, an unwillingness to accept what life and growth require.

Recognizing the uniqueness of everything we connect with, and of the connections themselves, can be the foundation for making our way through the loss. No one can tell us what someone or something meant to us. Only we can determine those meanings for ourselves and name our loss.

Expressing Our Feelings

In the second movement of grief we express whatever feelings and emotions are called forth when we acknowledge our losses.

As we acknowledge what we have lost, our grief seeks expression. Because many of us have learned to fear great emotion, because we fret that we will be out of control, because we have been taught not to "offend" others with emotional expressions, we lean towards damming the emotion that is straining to be released. However, the healthy and meaningful expression of our emotions facilitates our passage through the grief process.

A willingness to grieve or mourn is the only way we can incorporate our losses into our being and continue on with a healthy life. Because grief is painful, we are tempted to think that we can avoid it—and all of its attendant emotions. However, when we try to avoid our emotions, the need to grieve simply buries itself within us and emerges at some other time, perhaps when we have a new experience of loss. Then we may wonder why we feel so bad about something that was not that significant. If the feelings are pushed down too long, they often seek expression in unhealthy ways. Grief can sour into chronic anger, cynicism, and even violence.

Expressing our emotions is necessary to healthy grieving. Emotions are God-given gifts. They usually arise in us without conscious decision on our part. If we befriend our emotions, listen to them, and express them in appropriate and meaningful ways, we can learn a great deal about ourselves and move through our grief.

Choosing to Let Go

Finally, we grow through our grieving when we choose to change the things we do that keep us tied to the lost person or object. As we accommodate ourselves to our loss through intellectual honesty and emotional release, we might find that we need to change some of the ways we act.

For example, refusing for a long time to change a dead child's room or to give away any of his or her belongings can be a denial of the child's death. When the death is acknowledged and grieved, we can more freely behave in accord with reality. A parent may choose to give the child's belongings to needy children, even though the giving is emotionally painful.

Children who have lost their parents may at some point need to sort through the parents' belongings—selling some, giving some away, and discarding others. Selling the family house may be a final farewell both to the parents and also to the loss.

Using the Reflections in This Book

Each of the reflections in this book begins with an opening prayer that helps remind us of God's presence with us and focuses our reflection.

A story, mostly taken from the life experiences of my patients or others, follows the prayer. The story should help you tune in to your own story of loss, eliciting memories and emotions about similar losses in your own life.

The next section of each reflection is a commentary, followed by some reflection exercises. In working through an exercise, you may become aware that you have kept a loss on a strictly intellectual level. You may acknowledge it, but refuse any expression of your feelings. Some exercises may ask for more than you feel ready to handle. Be gentle with yourself and do not undertake any exercise that feels too difficult. In other words, use each reflection at the appropriate time for your grieving. From reflection to reflection, you will notice that the suggested exercises are similar, but each is tailored to a particular subject. The three-part movement of grieving is much the same no matter what the subject of our grief may be.

After the commentaries and exercises, a passage from the Bible and a brief closing prayer are offered for inspiration and consolation. You may want to read these after each period of reflection.

Most important, remember that your grieving is *your* grieving. Use the reflections to meet your needs. This is not a book you need to read from cover to cover. Use the reflections that help you. Save the others for a time when death and life call you to them.

Other Helps

Here are some other suggestions for using the material in this book.

Create a sacred space. Jesus said, "When you pray, go to a private place, close the door, and then pray to God who is right there with you. The all-seeing God will reward you" (adapted from Matthew 6:6). If candlelight and meditative music help you to focus, then use them to create a prayerful space.

Open yourself to the power of grieving. Every human experience, including grieving, has a religious dimension. Grieving can open your mind and broaden your vision. Be open to the ways that God is leading you through your grief. Your emotions are messages from God that can tell you much about your spiritual quest. Conscious grieving can strengthen your will to act. In prayerful grieving, God can touch your will and empower you to live more fully.

Preview each reflection before beginning. Through previewing a reflection you may find that its topic is not one that resonates with you. Or you may realize that it is important but that you are only in the early stages of the process. Do not try to use all the reflection exercises at one period. Take your time.

Try writing or journaling. Writing is a process of discovery. If you write for any length of time, stating honestly what is on your mind and in your heart, you will unearth much about the grief you are going through, the strength to cope with it, and more.

In particular, you might find writing letters and dialogues helpful. Many people who have lost loved ones, especially if important words were left unspoken, find that writing a letter to the loved one can be a way of finally saying what needed to be said.

Dialogues may include other people, pets, talents, a job, and so on. When you write dialogues, you try to view the world from another perspective. This might seem strange at first, but you may find helpful insights and a release from some unresolved tensions. Without worrying about correct grammar or spelling, try writing the dialogue like a play script. For instance, a dialogue with a lost job might begin like this:

Me: Where did I go wrong?
Job: Nothing went wrong with you. The only problem you had was becoming so identified with me.
Me: What do you mean? I could take or leave you.
Job: Sure you could. That's how come you're eating yourself up with anger.

If you have never used writing as a means of reflection, try it. Reserve a special notebook for your journal writing. If you desire, you can go back to your entries at a future time.

Rituals can help in the letting go. At some point—and you will know when the proper time is—you may want to let go of your grief with the help of a ritual. Some people find a fitting ritual in writing the name of the lost person, dream, talent—whatever—on newsprint and then burning it with incense while offering prayer. Other people find a helpful release in making painted paper boats with some memento of the loss and then sailing them down a stream or off into a lake.

Design your own ritual. Your ritual may include prayers, poems, music, but it should also include some action of letting go. Again, a ritual is not a quick fix to counteract grief, but it can be helpful. Grieving has its own tempo.

❖ What is your own style, the choices you tend to make, the way you express your grief, as you cope with the losses in your life?

❖ Has your style helped you in the past, or do
you find yourself still angry and upset, holding
on to lost things and people in your life?

Conclusion

Every loss—and its grief—presents us with choices. We
can choose to move through loss, feel all the pain, and
come out on the side of growth. We can refuse to acknowledge the loss, hold on to it, and repress our grief.
Or we can get so caught up in the grieving itself that we
refuse to move on, turning chronic grief into a lifestyle.

We have the opportunity to "have life abundantly,"
and to become our full self through all the experiences
of our life—happy and sad. God created us so that we do
not need to look outside of our own life for the ingredi-
ents for growth and fulfillment. We always have options:
we can face the losses that life presents, let them go, and
grow through grief; or we can refuse to let go, become
chronic grievers, and work against our own growth.

Waking up to the integral nature of loss in our life
does not mean we must like the loss or the pain that
comes with it. It simply means we must recognize the
way things are in this universe, acknowledge that our
life follows the same pattern as every other creature, and
respond with a fully human yes to the process.

"Blessed are those who mourn" (Matthew 5:4, NJB)
seems a puzzling statement when we are grieving. Bless-
edness and happiness, however, require completion,
wholeness, and integrity. Loss is an invitation into new-
ness, birth, and life. Indeed, the only way we arrive at
fullness of life is by making our way appropriately

through many losses. The only way that we "will be comforted" (which is the rest of the beatitude) is if we give ourselves over to grieving. Conscious, honest mourning leads to the comfort Jesus promised.

❖ Have there been experiences in your life in which you can truly see the pattern of loss as a steppingstone to growth or new life?

❖ Can you say yes to whatever is waiting to be mourned in your life?

Twelve Guides to Grieving

1. Not all loss is of the same magnitude or kind.
2. All loss can be the groundwork for new life.
3. Losses are unique to each individual, because we grieve both over the loss of what something meant to us as well as over the lost object itself.
4. Change always brings loss, even when the change is welcome.
5. As our losses are unique, so are our ways of coping with them.
6. Loss evokes a wide array of emotions, whether we admit them or not.
7. We will find the makings of ourself in our own history of loss, especially in the ways we have chosen to deal with it.
8. While we cannot control the losses we experience in life, we can choose what we do with them.
9. Suffering is a mystery. The Son of God endured suffering and death out of love for and solidarity with us, but he never explained why we suffer.

10. God's grace gives us the choice of transforming loss into abundant life.
11. The Spirit dwells within us, suffers with us, consoles us, and will guide us to resurrection.
12. Growthful grieving involves three movements:
    a. openly acknowledging what has been lost
    b. expressing our feelings as we acknowledge the loss
    c. choosing to change the things that keep us tied to the loss

Aging

❧

"Who is that old person in the mirror?..."

Opening prayer: Eternal yet ageless God, you love me with an eternal and unconditional love. Help me to look at myself and my life with your eyes. You love me at every stage of my life. Grant that I may openly trust in you and willingly change and grow through all the days of my life.

Story

"Every once in a while I can't believe it when I look in the mirror," Betty said. "I don't feel any particular age inside, but when I see myself in the mirror, I'm shocked! I can't help but think, 'Who *is* that old person?'"

Betty prided herself on staying active and involved in life. She battled to maintain a relative slimness and worked at living a fairly healthy lifestyle. Except for minor aches and pains, she had no history of serious illness. Even so, Betty grew increasingly aware of and amazed at the changes in her body as she aged. She tried to block out this recognition much of the time, but then she would be surprised at the aging person who stared back in dismay from her mirror.

Comparing notes with one of her friends, Betty remarked, "I joined an aerobics class, and I like it a lot. It just took me a little longer to work up to the pace of everybody else. But I look around at all the others who are younger than I am, and I can really see where I used to be. All those firm, strong bodies!"

Betty knew the changes that had gradually crept up on her were still happening. Her light hair and clear skin had always been her best features. Now she noted gray hair, wrinkles, and age spots, even though the deeper smile lines on her face did offset some of the effects of aging.

Because she read a lot, Betty kept her bifocals hanging around her neck, and she wondered how she had ever gotten along without them. They went with her now to restaurants so she could read the menu and to church for reading the hymnal. Reading street signs became a challenge, and the last time she renewed her driver's license, she had to use her glasses to read the eye chart. She could not play as much tennis as she used to or zip through a whole day of hard housecleaning without taking a break. When she was younger, she had always dived in, stayed with it, and just felt pleasantly tired at the end.

Recently a cashier at the movies asked Betty and her husband, Jim, if they were eligible for the "senior citizen" discount. While they liked the decreased price, the question was a blow to both of them. "Do we *look* that old?" they asked each other.

Betty acknowledged that she was better at many things now than she had ever been. She read avidly, was an adventuresome cook, and had taken up watercolor painting. In some ways, she had greater self-confidence. She appreciated many aspects of her life more than ever before.

At times, though, sadness would creep in and Betty would think about who and where she was in life, how so many people and so much that she'd known and loved were already gone, and that her life was probably more than half over. The fact that she would probably never do all the things she would like to do hit her hard. She would never again be the person she used to be. "How hard it is," Betty thought, "to grow older."

Commentary

Until we move into midlife, we act as though aging has nothing to do with us. We have a sense that aging creeps up on us and captures us when we aren't looking, somewhere around the age of forty. Even after that we do not really believe it for a while. We stay active and keep ourselves looking good. Nobody knows—especially us. Besides, we are still important to our families, and we have lots to do at work.

Every once in a while, however, the truth breaks through and reminds us that we are moving along. Life is doing what it does for every living creature—flowing without cessation until death. The awesome sense of our life's inexorable movement to the end begins to scare us.

Losses happen in our early years, but we blithely over-look them because so many new things come into our life. We relish growing up. During these early years, we know that death happens. Perhaps our grandparents die. People die in tornadoes, fires, and accidents. We might have to bury our deceased canary or beloved cat. But concern about our own death seldom surfaces.

Somewhere in the middle of our life, the fact of our own death sneaks—or sometimes storms—out of the closet. We have a hard time looking past the ways we are changing. We see wrinkling skin, graying hair, sag-ging muscles, and rapidly diminishing energy. We are horrified and, deep down, we are scared.

Confronted with our own demise, we want to rebel. Fortysomething men and women suddenly start aero-bics, brisk walks, and low-fat diets. While maintaining strength, good health, and a clean and attractive appear-ance is wise at any age, we might go to great lengths to maintain the illusion of youth even as it passes—some-times even after it is long gone. This is denial.

Having grown up in a culture that glorifies youth, we may have unconsciously and consciously adopted cul-tural values about the aging process. When we at midlife begin to pine for youth, we devalue who we are, as we are. Some of us become almost apologetic for our age.

By the middle of our life, losses come at an increas-ingly faster pace. Friends and family move off or are taken in death. Jobs change and retirement looms. Long-held dreams and hopes begin to lose any possibility of fulfill-ment. Our body gradually gives way to chronic ailments and conditions that we used to think only afflicted our elders. We are encountering our own vulnerability.

Too often, we spend our energy trying to make the losses of aging unreal. We gain nothing by pretending that aging is easy. In youth, change almost automatically meant gain. The formula was built into our developing body. In middle age and beyond, however, growth and gain are up to us. The first step in growing through our aging is to acknowledge the losses.

We open ourselves to opportunity when we are willing to look at the losses involved in our aging and to allow and accept all of the accompanying feelings. Nothing pushes us to try to make sense of life like aging, trying to find growth through diminishment.

Reflection Exercises

◆ As you settle yourself into a comfortable position, relax. Take some deep breaths and call on the Holy Spirit to be with you in your meditation. Imagine that you are watching a videotape recorded at all stages of your life, from baby pictures to pictures taken today. You control the speed of the video, so you advance it slowly. At key moments, you push the mental pause button and ponder how you looked, what you could do, how you felt.

When you turn off the mental video, write a list of all that you have gained and lost as you have aged. Check those losses that have been especially hard for you. Be aware of the emotions that arise with these thoughts and let them flow.

◆ Consider the images you have of beauty and goodness. How close are they to Madison Avenue types? Are your images making it difficult for you to accept your own aging? Is any change in image called for?

◆ Imagine a dialogue between the part of you that does not want to age and the part that is willing to accept aging. Write the dialogue in your journal. Then talk to God about what you discovered.

◆ Bring to mind the most difficult thing about being your present age. Ponder all the losses that are represented by your distress. Note the losses in your journal, along with the feelings that go with them. What is keeping you from letting your losses go and moving on? Do you want to move on? What would it take to do that?

◆ Imagine standing back and looking at your life from a distance. You see yourself at a place in the middle—some road already traveled and some yet to come. How do you want to live what is yet to come? What will help that happen?

◆ Picture yourself taking each loss into your hands, thanking whatever was lost for all it brought you, and setting it free. As you release each one, you may want to say something like, "I'm grateful for all the gifts you have given me, and in the name of my growth and movement in this life, I set you free and send you back to God from whom you came."

You may want to ritualize this setting free by writing your losses on pieces of paper, perhaps coloring them with watercolors or colored markers. Then, in a private place, pray and mourn out loud over each loss. Finally, burn your losses with some incense, thanking God for them and letting go.

◆ Pray with God's Word. Consider what brings "wisdom, stature, and favor" (Luke 2:52, NJB) with God and people.

God's Word

> *Charm is deceitful, and beauty empty;*
> *the woman who fears Yahweh is the one to praise.*
>
> —Proverbs 31:30, NJB

> *Ah, how goodness and kindness pursue me,*
> *every day of my life.*
>
> —Adapted from Psalm 23:6

> *Yahweh, I have trusted you since my youth,*
> *I have relied on you since I was born,*
> *You have been my portion from my mother's womb,*
> *and the constant theme of my praise.*
>
> —Adapted from Psalm 71:5–6

> *God, you taught me when I was young,*
> *and I am still proclaiming your marvels.*
> *Now that I am old and gray,*
> *God, do not desert me;*
> *let me live to tell the rising generation*
> *about your strength and power,*
> *about your heavenly righteousness.*
>
> —Adapted from Psalm 72:17–18

Closing prayer: O God, you continue to be with me throughout my aging, holding me in your hands as I struggle to grow in wisdom, in stature, and in favor with you. Let me attend to each day of my life and each age, living them fully, joyfully, and thankfully.

Relationships

"It's awful to feel so alone...."

Opening prayer: Gracious God, embrace me in my grieving over relationships that are lost. Grant me true gratefulness for the good that came to me through these significant people. Lead me through all the emotions that are likely to overwhelm me. Through your love, bring me to healing.

Story

Jackie and Kathy lived across the street from each other for twelve years. Their husbands jokingly suggested building an enclosed footbridge over the street to let the women go back and forth without coats in the winter and shoes in the summer. The women's relationship started to grow immediately after Jackie, Bill, and their family moved in. Kathy, seeing the kids, baked a batch of chocolate chip cookies and took them over that first afternoon.

Jackie welcomed Kathy and invited her to sit down for cookies and milk. They had been intimate friends ever since. "It was one of those times when you just click," Kathy said. "I could feel it right off. Jackie was my kind of person. Our kids were real close in age, too, except that Walt and I have three, and Jackie and Bill have two."

Having such a close friend was the greatest gift to Jackie. An only child, Jackie had always wanted a sister that she could tell everything to. Even without blood ties, Kathy fit the description better than anybody had ever done before, and Jackie was ecstatic. Through the years the women helped each other in hundreds of ways. When their kids were small, if one of the mothers had an appointment or wanted to go shopping, the other looked after all five children. They carpooled for everything from school to soccer games to dental appointments. As the kids became teenagers, the two women laughed and cried on each other's shoulders about their delights and distresses. The two families shared countless meals at each other's homes.

Squabbles and misunderstandings between the women were quickly patched up, and the two felt closer for the challenge. Although Walt and Bill never became as close as their wives were, the two men liked each other and the interplay of the two families. They knew they could count on each other for almost anything. What they did not count on was Bill's transfer to Los Angeles.

Jackie had been gone a year and a half, and Kathy was still not used to it. She remembered clearly the evening that Jackie came over with tears running down her cheeks and broke the news. "We have to take it," Jackie said through her tears. "Bill's orders are nonnegotiable. The company needs him to start a division out there like the one he runs here, and won't take no for an answer. With the kids almost ready for college, we can't afford to let go of the job."

No matter how many tears were shed, no matter how many wishes were made for the deal to fall through, the day arrived when Kathy, Walt, and the kids stood out on the street and waved forlornly as their closest friends drove off to California. After two months of astronomical phone bills, Jackie and Kathy decided they would have to cut back. Despite plans to get together in the months to come, to meet halfway, to vacation together, nothing had come about. Now they wrote on occasion, but it was just not the same.

Kathy still found Jackie's absence devastating. The new folks that moved into Jackie and Bill's house kept their distance. But, then, nobody could take Jackie's place. Jackie and she were soul mates. Kathy felt like part of herself had vanished. Even though her family and other friends were still close and loving, and even though she stayed busy, one day Kathy stood looking across at Jackie's house and heard herself say, "It's awful to feel so alone." She did not understand why she just could not shake the deep sadness and get on with her life.

Commentary

Relationships play a more significant part in our life than we sometimes realize. They become a part of our world and the fabric of our self.

When a significant relationship comes to an end, our grief can seem overwhelming, and its depth might surprise us. We may not realize how important a relationship is until we lose it. We chide ourselves for feeling so bad—"You'd think she died or something!" But the departure of a friend or breakup of a significant relationship truly is a form of death. None of us maintain all the relationships that we have ever formed, but something in us makes us try. Grade-school, high-school, and college friends—people who we swore would always be our most important friends—spread out across the country, and we lose contact. When we do see them again, perhaps at homecoming, we find ourselves talking to near strangers and wondering why our friends have changed so much. In our eagerness to accept a promotion, move into a new job, or retire, we discover that the casualties of change can include intimacy with important friends and the loss of valued co-workers.

Clearly, the circumstances surrounding the broken connection play a role in our healing. When the relationship is fractured through no fault of our own—as in Bill's job move in the opening scenario—sadness and loss seem to predominate. We feel the huge hole in ourself where the good friend used to rest. These losses do not confuse us. Although we do not like them, we understand them. Losses of this sort tend to heal more quickly, as the emotion is fairly clear, expected, and seems to arise naturally.

The acrimonious breakup of a marriage or long-term partnership can devastate us. In such circumstances, people sometimes make remarks like, "It would be easier for me if she had died. I thought all the hurt would be over once we'd broken up, but sometimes now it feels even worse." No matter how dreadful the marriage or partnership, the resultant anger, rage, guilt, sadness, and frustration can far outweigh the sense of relief.

When the other person chooses to break off a relationship because "I don't love you anymore" or "I found someone I prefer to be with," our self-esteem takes a beating. Besides feeling rejected as worthless, we are stormed by other chaotic emotions. The impulse to blame and attack the source of our pain intermingles with, and sometimes overpowers, our feelings of loss and sadness. At some point in our grief, we may begin to wonder what we did to bring about such rejection. Feelings of self-blame mix with anger, sadness, and depression.

Sorting through the feelings seems impossible. Even if we are the one who chooses to break up the relationship—even for good reasons—we may contend with our internal critic, who loads the blame on us. We may need to make our way through the memories of the relationship many times to confirm our choice to end it. We still need to grieve over what we lost.

Other emotions may complicate the experience of loss, especially fear—fear about handling financial challenges, about managing life on our own, about assuming total responsibility for children, about maintaining good relationships, and about spending the rest of our life alone.

No formal rituals are provided to help us with our grieving over the death of a relationship. In their efforts to console us, people may misguidedly congratulate us, say how smart we were to "get rid of" the person, and even tell us things about the other that we did not know. Rarely are we given the permission from others to express what we truly feel. The death of a relationship is a significant, powerful loss. We need to grieve for it in order to let go and be comforted.

Reflection Exercises

♦ Sit quietly, breathe deeply, and relax. Allow your body to sink into a comfortable position. Beginning with the most recent, identify significant relationships that you have lost through ways other than death. Go back in your life as far as you can remember. List the losses in your journal. Remember each person—how you met, what attracted you to each other, things you did together, the best and worst times of your relationship, and the ending. If you have pictures or artifacts that remind you of a person, find them and look at them to stimulate your recollection.

♦ As you write in your journal or reflect about these lost relationships, a particular loss may stir strong feelings. If so, spend time with that loss. Let your full range of emotions emerge, even those that are uncomfortable and that you tend to push away. Stay with the feelings.

If you feel like crying, cry. If you feel angry, find a way to express that anger—pound a pillow, write and then tear up or burn a letter to the person with whom you are angry, find a way to let the anger out nondestructively. It may be helpful to express these feelings to a caring, nonjudgmental person. When you feel ready and able to let go of some of the emotion, you may say a prayer like this: "O God, I release all my anger, pain, and sadness into your hands. Please help me with..."

You may need to repeat this exercise several times.

♦ Without worrying about how artistic you are, draw, paint, or color a picture of how you feel about the breakup of your relationship with a significant person. Compose the picture freely and spontaneously; do not censor yourself in any way. Do the picture at one sitting, expressing exactly how you feel at the moment.

When you finish, ponder what is expressed in the picture. Then put the picture away. Give yourself a few days, take the picture out, and reflect on it again. Ask yourself if you are ready to let go of this relationship and if there is anything preventing you from letting go. If you are ready to let go, use the picture in a ritual of release.

♦ Perhaps you are in the throes of emotion from a recently lost relationship. Try to be clear about what you have lost along with the relationship: position? prestige? security? companionship? connections? Attend to the emotions and what they may be expressing. Let them flow. Ask the Holy Spirit to be with you and grant you the grace to let go.

♦ Whether a relationship ended with distress or with poignant sadness and gratitude, each relationship gave you something positive. Consider your list of lost relationships again and ponder how each one helped to make you who you are at this moment. Pray for each person.

♦ Finally, pray with the awareness that everything in this world is passing, including important relationships. Ask for the gifts of appreciation and enjoyment of the relationships that are important at any moment in your life.

God's Word

Does a woman forget her baby at the breast,
or fail to cherish the child of her womb?
Yet even if these forget,
I will never forget you.
See, I have branded you on the palms of my hands.

—Adapted from Isaiah 49:15–16

Closing prayer: O God, every person who has been part of my life is still alive in me. Heal my hurt from broken relationships and sad partings. Thank you for all of the gifts that have come from significant persons. Help me to keep loving, even though I know how much love can cost.

REFLECTION 3

Jobs or Roles

"Nothing I do is important anymore...."

Opening prayer: Holy Friend, be with me as I grieve positions and roles that I have lost. After the recognition and the anguish, let me see beyond the grief to opportunity, and let me grow in faith and hope.

Story

Jeremy went into hospital administration for two reasons. He believed that he had the potential to be a good manager, and he wanted to help people in need. This aspect made his job more than "just a job" for him.

Over fifteen years, he advanced from his residency in hospital administration to positions with increasing responsibility. He constantly learned new skills and felt confident that he made some important contributions to his hospital. He settled into his job, believing that he would be there throughout his working life.

After years of relative stability, management of the hospital changed suddenly and traumatically for Jeremy. His contentment was swept away. New technology swiftly altered long-existing procedures and required skills that many of the older employees did not have. Paperwork burgeoned, but economic constraints set the number crunchers scrambling to downsize. No facet of the hospital's management was left unexamined and unscathed. As assistant administrator, Jeremy struggled to help the hospital staff navigate through these changes, but morale steadily sagged.

Then the bottom fell out for Jeremy. His position was eliminated in an effort to trim management. A younger, less expensive manager had to absorb Jeremy's workload. In what seemed like the bat of an eye, Jeremy was out.

At first Jeremy could not believe it. He had given his whole professional life to the hospital. He worked hard, did not complain about persistent overtime, and had even received awards for his excellent performance. The idea of working anywhere else was beyond imagining. Jeremy was part of this hospital. A huge hole opened up inside him where his work had been.

Anger boiled up in him. A torrent of accusations and questions fed his bitterness: This is what he got for being a good employee? This was his reward for loyalty? Jeremy directed a surge of vitriol at the remaining administrators. Why him and not them? Were they better than he was? Jeremy raged against the unfairness of life, the untrustworthiness of other people, even the seeming absence of God.

At the same time, personal questions nagged him: What did I do to deserve this? Was I as good as I thought

I was? Am I being punished for something? My family depends on me, and I've let them down. Will this change the way they feel about me? Have I been fooling myself about being competent? What on earth am I going to do now?

Jeremy began searching for a new job. Other hospitals were in turmoil, so he looked elsewhere. Not only was finding a job a struggle, but Jeremy also battled with his emotions and confusion. Before he could go out in the morning, Jeremy had to make his way through the heaviness of depression, helplessness, and dark questions about his worth. At odd times during the day, he found himself fighting back tears, and he would unexpectedly lash out in anger at his wife and children. Most of all, Jeremy was scared—scared that life would never be the same, that he could not take care of his family, and that no one would ever respect him again.

Commentary

Very early in life, we learn the importance of *doing*. In fact, our value is often tied to what we do. "Timmy, you're a bad boy—you spilled your milk." "What a wonderful girl Tracy is. She can dress herself!" Achieving good grades in school, sharing our toys, cleaning our room, and obeying our parents are ways to demonstrate that we are good people, worthy of love and praise.

Eventually many of us come to define ourself by what we do. We study, learn a trade, gather experience in some field, and tell ourselves and others, "I am a teacher," or "I am a personnel specialist," or "I am a priest," or "I am a mother," or "I am a plumber." Because we orient our life around doing, every time we meet someone new we quickly get to the question, "What do you do?"

To make our way in the world and to earn a living, we must pursue a job and assume roles. Of course, a job contributes to our own becoming fully human and to the well-being of society. In the best of circumstances, our doing—the work we do and roles we perform—contributes to our *being*. Our doing helps us to become ourselves and to develop our potential. Problems arise when we find our whole identity in what we do and then are stripped of our role or lose our job.

From the birth of her first child onward, nothing was as important to Sharon as being a mother. Her three children always came first. Being "mom" to them and their friends was the greatest of compliments. As each child grew up and left home, however, Sharon went into a tailspin. When the last one was about to leave, Sharon cried uncontrollably. She was shocked to realize that her children did not need her in the same way anymore. She confessed, "I feel useless. I hardly know who I am." "Mother" had become Sharon's primary identity, and when her children left home, she felt that she had been fired.

Similar cries are heard from many retirees. Almost all retired folks tell us what they used to do. A famous college football coach declared at his televised retirement party that football was his life. One month later his sudden death stunned the sports world and left many people wondering if when he stopped coaching he had stopped living. When retirement comes, we may discover that we feel stripped of our identity, and we don't know how to just *be*. Our job was more than a way of expressing our being—it *was* our being.

When our job or roles carry such power with us as to be our very identity, we need to grieve the losses of these roles. Telling ourselves that we shouldn't feel bad, rationalizing that our grown children's departure will give us more time for ourselves, or saying "just enjoy your retirement" does not begin to heal the loss of our jobs or roles. Indeed, many of us may not even recognize how deeply we identify with our jobs or roles until we lose them.

Sadness, depression, guilt, shame, fear, and helplessness may hit us. Anger may erupt if others have been the source of us losing our job or our role. Expressing these feelings plays an important role in grieving over the loss of a job or role.

Pondering the meaning of what we do now can prepare us to cope with the loss of a job or role in the future. We can try to discover what our jobs or roles mean to us. We can ask ourselves: Is my job central to my life? Are my roles who I am?

Our major concern should be how much value we assign to what we do in relation to who we are. After all, we tend to play down everything else that makes us who we are. One of my clients commented about her diabetes: "I was thinking about all this after I was diagnosed, and I decided something. I never call myself a diabetic because that sounds like it's my whole identity, and it colors everything about me. It feels more correct for me to say 'I have diabetes.'" Just as my client is not "a diabetic," no one is *only* a teacher, a nurse, a truck driver, a flight attendant, or whatever. We are always more than one aspect of ourselves.

After we have acknowledged our loss of a job or an important role and expressed our feelings about it, the next step in our grieving is to begin saying something like, "There's more to me. Those are things I do and do well, but they aren't the whole of me. I'm also an artist, sports fan, good friend, singer in the church choir, mountain biker, dancer, spouse, child—a many-faceted human being. My being before God is my most important identity. All the things I do are only important if they help me be the person God created me to be."

Like other losses, the loss of a job or role affects us as a whole person but also provides us with an opportunity to grow and develop our sense of self in a much broader context. By acknowledging the reality of such losses, and how deeply we are affected by them, we can move through them. We can remove their power to immobilize us and undermine our sense of self.

Reflection Exercises

♦ Call to mind any jobs or roles you may have lost or outgrown. How do these losses affect you now? Do you still hold any of the feelings that were there when the losses happened? What are those feelings? Let them arise in you naturally.

♦ If one loss is particularly fresh, spend additional time with it. Acknowledge what you have lost, what effects the loss is having on you, your relationships, and other aspects of your life. Be open to any feelings of shame, anger, hurt, fear, and so on, that need to be expressed. If you find it helpful, release your emotions on paper through writing or drawing.

Spend time with Jesus, pouring out your grief over this loss. Hold nothing back. Ask for his healing and help.

◆ Take some deep breaths and ask the Spirit to be with you in your reflection. Start listing on paper, perhaps in your journal, all the roles and jobs you identify with in your life. Let your mind travel in all directions. It may be helpful to begin each one with "I am…" For example, "I am a husband, I am a father, I am an insurance salesman, I am a football fan," and so on.

After listing as many roles and jobs as come to mind, you may want to rank them in order of importance. These questions might help you establish the importance of a particular role or a job: How much do I think about this role or job when I am not actually doing it? How many other parts of my life would be affected by any change in this job or role?

Once you have completed the list and rating, ponder what you have written. Is there anything surprising about your list? What is gratifying about it? What is disappointing? Do you want to change anything on your list?

◆ If one loss has been especially hard to let go of, reflect on what keeps you from moving on. What do you get out of holding on? Are unexpressed feelings holding you back? Have you placed some false hopes in the way, like thinking that perhaps you will get the job back? Are you still so angry at people that you cannot let go? Meditate on this situation and these questions. Pray for God's light to lead you past the blockages to growth and release.

◆ Have any losses in the past opened new avenues for you? Have you come to know yourself in new ways since those experiences? How did they push you to stretch yourself? Talk to God or dialogue in your journal about these losses and what their effects were.

◆ Slowly and thoughtfully repeat the following prayer, based on God's Word. Pause between each repetition and let the words settle into your soul: "God's love for me is a free gift that comes without my earning it."

God's Word

> *The power of God...has saved us and called us to be holy—not because of anything we ourselves have done but for [God's] own purpose and by [God's] own grace.*
>
> —*2 Timothy 1:9,* NJB

Closing prayer: O God, you love me freely. Let my work and all my doing help me to find my identity in you. Thank you for my ability to work and to enjoy it. Heal me of any bitterness about losses of roles, and may I let go of my losses and be open to new growth. May my doing be woven into a unique, beautiful, generous, and fulfilling fabric of life.

REFLECTION 4

The "Good Old Days"

"If only things could be like they used to be...."

Opening prayer: O God of my past, my present, and my future, help me to live in this moment and not try to escape into the past. Let my memories, both pleasant and painful, be steppingstones to wholeness. You are here now with me, loving God.

Story

The stiff white sheets felt rough under her hands as Margaret waited for the nurse to come back. In all her seventy-nine years, Margaret had only been in the hospital once before, and she did not want to be here this time. During each previous illness or injury, Margaret had been able to take care of herself and her family at home. In fact, she relished knowing that she did a pretty good job of it too, but that was with the help of Dr. Williams. How she missed him!

Dr. Williams had always come to the house. He had
delivered all four of Margaret's babies and treated her
husband in his last illness. She counted on Dr. Williams
for her family and knew he counted on her to care for
them. He had said many times, "Margaret, what would
I ever do without you?" She did not have any training,
but he would always show her what to do, and she would
do it.

Margaret could talk with Dr. Williams, and he would
listen. Like the time she got a funny feeling about the way
the first of her babies was acting, and she called for the
doctor. He did not argue—he just came out to the house.
A good thing, too, because the baby was coming down
with pneumonia and burning with fever. Dr. Williams
directed Margaret to give the baby cool baths—without
which, chances are, he never would have made it.

Now Margaret was frightened and upset with herself. Dr. Williams had died twelve years ago, and she
had not seen a doctor since. If she had not fallen off the
kitchen chair, she would not be in the hospital this time.
All the comings and goings of the emergency room bothered Margaret's sense of order and control.

After she arrived at the emergency room, Margaret
had to wait two hours for any care. Only the ambulance
attendant listened when she complained of the pain in
her hip. The shot he gave her helped some. Other patients in the emergency room were yelling with pain and
crying. Nurses just rushed past her. When she asked what
was wrong with her, they briskly announced that her hip
was fractured, and she would need surgery. This news—
and the confusion—frightened Margaret.

Once Margaret got to her room, the quiet calmed her

a little. The nurse who checked her in was friendly. Margaret hoped she would see her again. Even so, after quick visits by three different doctors in the emergency room and the x-rays, she felt cross-examined, poked, and prodded. The doctor scheduled to do her surgery was a total stranger. Being in the hands of an unknown doctor scared Margaret.

As Margaret waited for the surgeon, she wished things could be like they used to be! Simpler. People really cared about one another then. People listened to her. She knew her doctor. Even though he did not have all the medicines and things they had now, he did a good job and was there for her. Most of the time she could stay at home. Now everything felt so coldly impersonal.

Nostalgia for the way things used to be frequently welled up in Margaret. Pleasant memories flooded back. The visits of Dr. Williams, and his wonderful reassurances. Doing just simple little things. Not having to spend money to have a good time. The clothes they wore back then. "Why couldn't things just stay the way they were?" she murmured to the empty room. "Oh, for the good old days."

Commentary

Tender or triumphant recollections can be a source of support and consolation. Indeed, we see the hand of God in our life mostly through hindsight. With all of its ups and downs, our story, when recollected in tranquillity, can remind us of valuable lessons learned. Laura, a client of mine, commented "You know, for years I've been working in the city, but my memories of growing up in the country are really alive, and they help me relax when things get hectic!" Memories tell us where we have been and who we are.

When old friends get together, nearly every sentence begins with "Remember when..." Families have favorite stories that are told over and over. Jim, another client, commented that "I was never really aware of how much Mike, my brother, meant to me until I started thinking about our times together as kids." Reminiscing can teach us the value of something that was taken for granted, providing us with a second chance to gather the gifts of our experience.

At other times, we may be totally unaware of the impact that something or someone had on us. Only later, as we remember and mull over what happened, does its significance become apparent. However, these same memories have the power to prevent us from living in, and dealing with, the present.

We are bombarded with change and novelty. In this whirlwind, we may be tempted to seek a secure and steady place, a simpler time. We may return in our minds to a time when we were comfortable, relatively happy, and not weighed down with responsibility. Such dreaming is a natural coping reaction.

Another way to avoid dealing with the present is to languish amid problems and pain from the past. We grasp painful memories as an excuse for our current difficulties. Most of us have heard other people—and maybe even ourself—say something like, "My mother never understood me. Why, I remember the time...and that's why I'm not successful now."

When we habitually dwell in memory, when we constantly repeat old stories not for their wisdom but as a way of shielding ourselves from the present, we are trying to control our life. But this is a grand illusion. Life will not come under human control. To live fully means to be open to the shock of events. To dwell in the past is to disallow adventure in our life, because adventure requires that we sally forth into the world *as it is now.* Dwelling in the past puts blinders on our eyes, so that we cannot see the full range of life's possibilities.

More important, the God of surprises and miracles will not come under our control either. God is the eternal present who invites us to encounters *now.* If we dwell in memory, we miss God's present invitations to growth and renewal.

To grieve the "good old days" or the "bad old days" and let go of them, we need to ask ourselves: What is it that pushes me to hold on to some memories and not others? Why do I selectively zero in on a certain dress, toy, or reprimand and forget other clothes, toys, and praise? Why do I need to keep replaying the past? What am I afraid of in the present?

How we use our memories and reminiscences is up to us. When we cling to the past—for reasons of security or avoidance of the present—we may prevent ourself from making the most of what is. Growth can only take place in the present, because the present is all we ever really have. Letting go of the "good" or "bad old days" may be painful, but it may be a path toward the loving God who will come to greet us.

Reflection Exercises

◆ Quiet yourself, relax, and breathe deeply. In your journal or on a piece of paper, list the things about the "old days" that you still regularly bring to mind, cherish, and wish for, or use as excuses and hide behind. To facilitate your review, recall particular key events or dreams of yours from the first ten years of your life, the next ten years, and so on in ten-year increments. Then, write your reflections on these following questions:

❖ Do your wishing for and reminiscing about these days help you in your daily life, or do they mostly cause you to regret that things are not that way anymore?

❖ Are there certain times when you find yourself retreating to the "good old days" in your mind? Do specific experiences or problems trigger your retreat? If so, what experiences or problems? What do those memories help you to avoid?

Ask God for the graces you need to let go of the "good" and "bad old days" that you hold on to.

◆ Is there a common theme or thread in your reminiscing? Are all of your memories about warmth and closeness? being taken care of? having no responsibility? the ways that life was unfair? What can you learn about your present life from this common theme or thread? How can you let the memories go so they do not affect the present in negative ways?

◆ When you find yourself reminiscing about happier, warmer times, you might offer this prayer: "God, I am grateful for the blessings that have been part of my life. I am especially grateful for... May I use these blessings to enrich my life and the lives of other people. Help me to embrace the present."

◆ If you find you spend a lot of time regretting that things are not like they used to be, you may want to follow these steps:

❖ Call to mind all those things that you miss about the past.
❖ Thank God for blessings that accompanied or came through these remembered gifts.
❖ Note any aspect of the "old ways" that could remain in your life in a healthy way and how you might further integrate it into your way of life.
❖ Consider what life may be asking you to release from the "old days."
❖ Allow yourself to experience whatever feelings of sadness or regret that surface.
❖ Plan what you will do when these old thoughts come up and you are tempted to stay with them. Your plan may include, for example, a quick prayer, such as "God, thanks for so many good things in my past. Help me to make today a day that I'll also love to remember."

◆ Ritually turn over unserviceable dreams and nostalgia to God. Include a ritual action, prayer, and perhaps a favorite hymn.

God's Word

Now is the favorable time; this is the day of salvation.

—*Adapted from 2 Corinthians 6:2*

This is the day made memorable by Yahweh.
Let us rejoice and be glad!

—*Psalm 118:24*, Psalms Anew

Closing prayer: My God, present now, teach me to see how good today is. While I thank you for my past and all the gifts I have received, help me to live mindfully in the present and to recognize the ways you come to me in every moment.

Significant Objects

"I feel as if I lost Grandpa all over again...."

Opening prayer: Loving God, grant that I may see the full extent of your gifts to me and understand how much they mean to me. May I treasure and enjoy these gifts while I have them and then let them go. I give you thanks for your great goodness.

Story

One of Jim's earliest memories was of being snuggled in grandpa's lap, grandpa's strong arms holding Jim close against a soft flannel shirt. Grandpa was always there to talk with, cry to, be hugged by, even to argue with sometimes. Amid the turmoil of his childhood, Jim depended on his grandfather's love, steadiness, and wisdom.

Even when Jim moved on to college and, afterwards, to other adventures, even though he loved and was loved by other people, his grandpa was home base. Despite his

diminishing energy and increasing age, Jim's grandpa
played a powerful and vibrant role in Jim's life.

When his grandfather died, Jim was out of the country on business. Though the death was anticipated, it
still came as a shock. Jim knew he had lost the one solid
rock at the center of his world. The loss devastated Jim.
During the pain and grief, a family member handed
grandpa's ring to Jim and said, "He specifically told me
that he wanted you to have it, Jim." Jim felt an inex-
pressible wave of love and gratitude sweep through him.

The worn gold ring with its dark red stone had been
a part of his grandpa's hand—Jim had never seen his
grandfather without it. As a tiny child in grandpa's lap,
Jim had played with the ring, twisting it around to hide
the stone, telling Grandpa it was gone. And Grandpa
always played along, feigning distress, wondering, "Who
took that stone?" and finally showing surprise and delight when little Jim made it "come back."

Jim broke into loud sobbing when he was handed the
ring. He held it tightly and finally slipped it on, suddenly
feeling Grandpa holding him close once again. Later, Jim
confessed that, above all, the ring helped him make his
way through the painful grief.

One day, about two years after his grandfather's death,
Jim returned to his home to find his belongings ransacked.
Jim hurried through the apartment, almost ignoring the
vacant spots where his television and stereo had been. He
searched for one treasure, the ring. When he got to the
chest of drawers, his heart sank. Searching desperately
through the small drawer, Jim could not find his grandfather's ring. Groping around on the floor, he prayed that
the thieves had overlooked so small an item. Finally, the

sad truth crushed him. Grandpa's ring was gone. He wept as he did at his grandfather's funeral. When he told the story of the theft, he always shook his head, stifled tears, and said, "It felt like I'd just lost grandpa all over again."

Commentary

Not every possession is precious to us. We could give away some of our belongings in a moment, without regrets or feelings of loss. Sorting through our possessions to find out what is significant can prove to be a fascinating exercise. We might discover that odd things hold enormous meaning for us: the sweater made by someone dear, the A+ paper from a favorite teacher, the chewed collar that Rex wore. Some of these belongings become priceless. Our inclination is to cling to them forever.

Objects become precious because we connect them to special persons or to key experiences in our life. They become part of our identity. In fact, some things may be cheap, even tacky, but we may assign meaning to them that attaches them to our heart.

Bill, Marjorie's journalist husband, worked many years on an ancient manual typewriter. It had become the joke of his coworkers, who watched him peck away at the worn keys with surprising rapidity. Offers to replace the vintage typewriter with an electric model or even a word processor were rejected outright. Bill clung tenaciously to his old typewriter. "It's been through the wars with me," he liked to say.

After Bill's sudden, fatal heart attack, Marjorie collected all his belongings from work. She gave many of his things to friends, but she could not bear to part with the typewriter. When she finally relinquished it, Marjorie felt like she was giving Bill away.

We might tend to minimize the loss of "things," and sometimes we do not understand just what we are grieving over. We will hear ourself saying things like, "I don't know what's wrong with me, why I'm so upset over that silly pen I lost." However, the monetary value has little to do with our feelings about the lost item if our heart has assigned value to it. When the possession we lose is connected with a personal achievement, we may find ourselves feeling diminished.

On finishing a graduate degree in architecture, Doug and his classmates each received a slide rule from the department head. From the day that Doug began work, he used that slide rule to measure every angle, room, and dimension. It became an extension of his hand. Even though he had moved on to using computers, when the slide rule was accidentally discarded with a group of papers it had nestled between, Doug felt helpless. Nothing worked as well. Insecurities about his skill as an architect cropped up. Eventually he realized that he had to get beyond his grief, but it still took time before he regained his confidence.

Like Bill's typewriter or Doug's slide rule, some possessions give us a sense of knowing where we came from. They ground us in our own history. When we lose these reminders, we may feel like we have lost part of ourselves, and we ache with and need to grieve over the loss.

When the lost item stirs up unfinished grieving over the death or loss of someone dear, we may want to focus on the person the object represented. When the lost item is connected to other losses, we may help ourselves by consciously becoming aware of whatever feelings we experience. As we recognize what we are feeling, the reality of what an object represented to us may emerge. Our grief can then be focused on a clearer appreciation of whatever meaning an object held for us. The opportunity this loss presents may also allow us to do unfinished grieving over other losses.

Reflection Exercises

♦ Relax into a comfortable position, taking deep, slow breaths to release any tension. Continue to breathe easily and slowly. Bring to mind the possessions that are especially dear or important to you. Make a mental note of each one. Then begin to recall other belongings that have been important in the past, but that you no longer have. Be aware of those that did not leave your possession easily—you may still carry distress or pain at their loss. List these losses in your journal and be aware of your emotions as you write. Let the feelings emerge.

♦ If thoughts of one lost object hold greater distress than any of the other losses, you may want to focus on that one object. Bring that precious belonging back to memory as clearly as you can. Meditate on these questions:

❖ What meaning did the object really hold for you, what did it represent to you?
❖ What do you feel you lost besides the object itself?
❖ How does that loss still have meaning for you?

As these thoughts come together, ask the Holy Spirit to accept that precious belonging as a gift from you, along with all the sadness and other feelings that are tied to it. If a ritual would help your letting go, perform an appropriate action.

◆ Look over the list of significant things that you have lost or released in your life and think about how you have managed to let go. What has been your typical way or style of getting through loss? Has it been healthy and helpful to you? Or do you tend to act like it doesn't matter and bury the loss deep inside? Has your method of getting over loss been effective?

◆ If you have a special place in your home that is your prayer place, or a spot outdoors that you find conducive to prayer, take to this place your list of all the precious belongings you no longer have. Let the list represent all your pain and sadness at the loss of those objects. Place the list on the sacred spot and pray: "God, as a sign of my desire to release any heaviness that holds me back or keeps me low in spirit, I thank you for these gifts, and now I give them back to you. May my memories of them be full of gratitude and joy."

◆ Ponder God's Word and think about what possessions you cling to now. Talk with God about them.

God's Word

> *Since we are justified by faith, we have peace with God through...Jesus Christ, through whom we have obtained access to this grace in which we stand;...we also boast in our sufferings, knowing that suffering produces endurance, and endurance produces character, and character produces hope, and hope does not disappoint us, because God's love has been poured into our hearts through the Holy Spirit that has been given to us.*

> —*Romans 5:1–5*, NRSV

Closing prayer: Creator of all good gifts, I come with gratitude for the many gifts that have come into my life. Receive from me all those that are no longer in my keeping, and give me a spirit that does not cling to those I still enjoy. Let me be aware that nothing is lost, that everything that is exists in you. Your reign in my heart is the treasure I seek.

REFLECTION 6

Death of a Loved One

"I don't think I can go on without him...."

Opening prayer: Living God, you created us to love one another. When a loved one dies, the pain staggers us and tests our faith. Help me in my grieving—in the outpouring of sorrow, of anger, of all my feelings, and in the letting go. Remind me that even Jesus wept when he was grieving and that his Resurrection has conquered death.

Story

At his usual time, Tom kissed his wife, Marilyn, and their daughter, Julie, good-bye and drove off to work. Marilyn rushed to get herself ready for work and Julie set for preschool. They left home shortly after Tom, and the day was on its way.

By the time Marilyn reached her office, Tom had been killed. While waiting at the stoplight of a busy intersection at the bottom of a hill, he became the stationary target for an out-of-control eighteen-wheeler with no brakes. Tom's car exploded into flames upon impact. By the time the fire was finally extinguished, Tom's body was almost unidentifiable. Thus, just as Marilyn was leaving work to pick up Julie, the police finally reached her with the horrible news.

Only much later could Marilyn speak clearly about that day. In an instant, her world collapsed. For days she walked around in numb shock. Tom's funeral passed in a blur of tears and periods of disbelief. Only Julie could break into her mother's awareness, but Marilyn would simply hold her and sob.

Eventually Marilyn's numbness lifted, but the emotional—and even physical—pain intensified. The truth that Tom would never come back began to sink in. Even so, sometimes she caught herself waiting for Tom, listening for his phone call, watching the door when he usually came home from work. She told me, "I didn't think I could take it. Each time the reality that Tom was gone hit me all over again. A wave of pain overwhelmed me. I thought I was dying myself. Sometimes I even thought about killing myself because it was too much to take. I don't know how many times I said to myself and even to my mother, 'I don't think I can go on without him.'"

Marilyn described her feelings as a "hodgepodge" during those months. Anger would flare up as she thought of the truck driver. "Sometimes I wished he had died. Or I wanted him punished, even though I later knew he wasn't really at fault." At other times Marilyn could not believe how angry she felt with Tom for leaving her and Julie. "Didn't he know we needed him?" Then she would feel guilty about her anger at Tom.

Marilyn fretted over what she wished she had said to him. She thought about what she could have done to prevent the accident. She vacillated between feeling furious with God, to pleading for God's help, to wondering why God was punishing her.

Only after many months of crying, talking, praying, jogging, and, finally, participating in a bereavement support group did Marilyn begin to feel herself coming back to life. "I didn't know for a long time who I was anymore. I was so connected to Tom—he was always there and felt like part of me—that with him gone, I didn't even feel like myself."

Commentary

Nothing throws us off balance like the death of someone important to us. From the day we are born, we live in relationship with other people and come to know who we are through these relationships. In fact, we learn early in life that our very existence depends on our connections with others. Our parents name us, care for us, and teach us how to behave. Our siblings and relatives tell stories about when we were small. We spend a lifetime making connections and defining ourselves through our relationships.

The relationships we hold dearest have the most profound effect on us, particularly when we lose them. The death of a loved one can disrupt our whole sense of self. Two months after the death of his wife, one man told me: "I feel like my whole self has been thrown up into the air and is floating down in little pieces. I don't know yet how the pieces will come back together."

We might avoid our grief because we do not want to

be a burden, and because we desire to just get on with our life. However, when we hold back on our grief and prevent ourselves from feeling its pain and sadness, it may bury itself within us. Grief is always pushing to express itself when we least expect it, particularly when other losses happen. When we refuse to grieve, we do not allow our healing.

Some understanding of what we might experience and how we might make our way through the loss of a loved one can help us grieve well. After all, such a loss affects every part of our being. Many of my patients have been frightened by the intensity of their grief. After some bereavement work, a newly widowed woman said: "I'm so glad I understand it better. I felt so bad and didn't know other people felt the same way. I thought I was going crazy."

When someone important to us dies, we live through the common experience of human grief in a uniquely individual style. In addition, the manner of the death influences the progress of our grieving. Grieving after a loved one's long, painful death has some different features than grieving a sudden and unexpected death. Grieving the death of a child may be quite different from grieving the death of an elder.

Our feelings of sadness, anger, and guilt can become so intense that they scare us. One client's remark typifies what many grieving people say: "I'm afraid that once I start crying, I'll never be able to stop." During intense emotions, we fear being out of control and may see emotions as enemies. People may sometimes tell us things like "Don't cry" or "Don't sit around feeling sorry for yourself. Just get busy, and it'll keep your mind off your troubles." So we may be tempted to stifle the expressions of our grief.

Our emotions are not our enemies. Emotions help us to express the depth of our pain and grief. They help us communicate our distress to others and allow them to know our struggles. Just as an infant's tears tell the parents that he or she is distressed, so do our adult emotions allow us not only to release our distress but also to reach out to others for support.

Jesus' tears over the death of his friend Lazarus can serve as a powerful example for us in our own grief. Jesus was "greatly disturbed in spirit and deeply moved ...[and] began to weep" (John 11:33–35, NRSV). Jesus wept because he loved Lazarus. Even though he knew that he could raise Lazarus from the dead, Jesus honored his friend with his grief and his tears. We honor our lost loved ones when we pour out our tears.

Our immersion into the reality of loss leads to intense feelings that invite us to struggle with our questions and to move on to new life. Nevertheless, we can refuse to grieve completely over the death of someone we love. We can hang on to our sadness and anger, or try to talk ourselves out of our painful feelings. We may choose to keep ourselves so busy that the feelings do not have time to emerge. By refusing to let go, we turn our grief into a lifestyle. In effect, we choose to let the loss overwhelm us. We choose a kind of death in life.

Though the intensity of our feelings usually tapers off, grieving over the loss of an important person may continue for several years. Anniversaries and holidays may be especially poignant times; little things may trigger our grief. As with all types of grieving, we can choose to grieve well by fully acknowledging the death of our special person, releasing our emotions, and then consciously, although gradually, letting go.

Reflection Exercises

◆ Relax and breathe deeply. Ask the Holy Spirit to be with you in your reflection. Allow any grief over the death of a loved one to come to the surface. Do not push it away. Name the person whose death evokes your grief. Invite memories of this person's life. Recall the good times and the bad. Attend to any emotions that come with these memories. Reverence the loved one by releasing your feelings. Then ask the Holy Spirit to breathe comfort into your heart.

◆ When any unfinished business arises—words that were not said, sorrow for pain or other relationship problems, anything you wish you had or hadn't done—choose a way to express it. Imagine yourself sitting with the person who has died. In a written dialogue, tell that person about your regrets. In your imagination, hear what that person would say in response to you. Writing down this dialogue may be helpful. Or let the ideas and emotions come to your mind and then write a letter to the person who has died, saying all the things you would still like to say.

◆ If anger toward God arises because God did not save the person from death or prevent great suffering, or if you feel unable to pray, or if God seems uncaring of your sadness, loneliness, or pain, do not push these feelings away. Instead, tell God exactly what your thoughts and feelings are. Cry or shout them out. Let them all flow openly. When you feel that you have expressed all you want to express, take some deep breaths and quiet yourself for a while. Listen to what your heart tells you.

◆ Call to mind all the ways you feel alone without the presence of the person who has died. Offer them consciously to God. You might say, "O God, … was a wonderful gift to me. Take my empty feelings now and fill them with your presence. And in your presence help me feel the love and presence of …. Let me know and feel that I am never truly alone."

◆ An accompanying ritual may help you let go. For example, if you have some memento of the person, you may want to leave it at the loved one's grave. Or if you still have many objects that belonged to the loved one, select those that you would like to keep as a reminder of the person, give the others away to people who could use them, or to other close friends or family members. Take your time sorting; remember the person and offer a prayer of thanks for that person as you dispose of each object.

◆ If you are having an especially hard time letting go of your grief, meditate on these questions:

❖ If my loved one were here in my place, what advice would she or he give me? What would that person want for me right now?
❖ Have I made grieving for … a lifestyle? If so, what holds me there?

❖ What practical matters do I now have responsibility for since ... is gone? Do I feel any aver-
sion to this responsibility? How can I assume—
or let go of—that responsibility now?

Then, in Jesus' name, ask God for the grace to let go
of the person. Offer the loved one to God, entrusting
him or her to God's care and to the communion of
saints—the Great Cloud of Witnesses.

◆ Pray with God's Word. Let the meaning of the passages assist you in your grieving.

God's Word

*Then I heard a loud voice call from the throne,
"God lives among people in this City. Here is God's
home. These people are God's. The Creator will
wipe away all their tears. Death will be no more.
Grieving and sadness will vanish."*

—*Adapted from Revelation 21:3–4*

*Happy are those who mourn, they shall be com-
forted.*

—*Adapted from Matthew 5:5*

Happy you who weep now: you shall laugh.

—*Adapted from Luke 6:21*

Closing prayer: O God, you know my sadness and loss and how hard it is to let go. I place my grief into your hands. Take all of my feelings, all of my loneliness and aching, all of my lack of understanding, and all of my yearning; transform these feelings through your love for me. Bring me to a place of comfort where my tears will be no more.

Abilities and Skills

"I feel like such a klutz...."

Opening prayer: Holy Friend, thank you for all the ways you allow me to be a unique manifestation of you. Let me learn and develop many skills and abilities, and then be willing to let them go when they have run their course and are no longer useful. Help me grieve the loss of abilities and skills that are no longer needed, but are begging to be kept.

Story

Dr. Wallace had always prided himself on his medical knowledge and skill. His patients knew that they had one of the best. Colleagues had frequently called on him for assistance when they were puzzled about a patient's condition. Although his personal style was gruff, he delighted in the confidence others placed in him.

But new technology and new modes of treatment had

changed medicine, moving beyond what Dr. Wallace knew well. His expertise still had a place, but he was passed over in critical cases. The younger doctors arrived with the latest training, and more specialists were appearing on the staff.

Dr. Wallace read everything he could, but he frequently ran out of time, with patients to see in his office and several hospitals to visit every day. He stayed with his patients though, even when they needed referrals to specialists.

The changing technology tested Dr. Wallace. His gruffness increased as he struggled to maintain his self-esteem. Although he never mentioned it to anyone, he gradually began to feel inadequate. The normal pressures of doctoring were a burden; now he also had to contend with the stress of his doubts and frustrations.

Finally, matters rudely came to a head. One of his longtime patients was admitted through the emergency room to intensive care in severe respiratory distress. Dr. Wallace rushed to the hospital. After checking his patient, he began reviewing the orders written by the emergency room doctor. He was brought up short by a question from his patient's nurse. "Dr. Wallace," she said, "are you going to call a doctor to see your patient?"

"I knew what she meant," he said later. "They're so used to dealing with specialists with all their patients, that she wondered who I might ask to consult. But the way she said it—and she's not even half my age, just a smart kid of a nurse—made me feel like I was worthless. *I'm* a doctor. In her one question, she rubbed salt in the wound I had been feeling for a long time. In fact, the wound keeps getting deeper and deeper. As hard as I try

to stay current and up to date, I feel like such a klutz.
I'm not sure if I should even try to keep on. Maybe my
time has run out."

Commentary

To be competent means having the requisite, adequate,
or suitable abilities for a task. Earning a living requires
competencies, but we need skills in other areas of life as
well.

Some men are great fathers because they have a special ability to nurture and relate to children. Competent
homemakers may develop a wide variety of abilities: planning parties, sewing, decorating, repairing, baking, and
entertaining guests. Athletes have to develop requisite
aptitudes. Other competencies and skills may fall into
the realm of "He can repair any piece of equipment you
take to him" or "She's really great at training animals."

We can usually find some arena in which our abilities
are accepted and valued. When we come into contact
with other people who have the same abilities, we find
an almost automatic camaraderie. Our skills give us an
identity with others. We also link our competencies to
who we are and to our sense of worth.

Once we gain competence in a particular area—and a
sense of belonging there—we tend to think that our place
is assured. However, deluges of fresh information and new
ways of doing things confront and challenge every person. As Dr. Wallace realized, the field of medicine has
grown to such a degree that specialty areas are being di-
vided into subspecialties. We have passed through agri-
cultural and industrial revolutions. Some commentators

have described our civilization as going through a "third wave": the information revolution. With oceans of new data and technology crashing down on us, it's easy to feel distressed and disoriented.

Most of our feelings of diminishing abilities come to us gradually. As advances in our field of expertise develop, we begin to feel like we are slipping. Ironically, sometimes our competence is the very reason we get behind. Competent people are rewarded for repeating acts of competence over and over again. Too often this means that we do not have incentives or time to renew our skills and information. Then it slowly dawns on us that a lot of our hard-won and serviceable knowledge and abilities are becoming obsolete.

Nothing remains the same. Knowledge by its nature is dynamic. Having good people skills, being adaptable, and being a good planner, mediator, and organizer will never lose value. However, even these skills may be challenged by change. For instance, a man may have great fathering skills when his children are young. Once they reach adolescence, however, he may feel that he has lost his ability to be a good father. Because of his teenagers' changing developmental needs and the pressures they face from their peers, they may challenge their father in ways he had never encountered. His basic abilities and experience, however, may still serve him well—with some minor adaptations.

Competence and skill in many aspects of life are subject to the same process as the rest of life—they come to birth, they develop, and they die. As with all grieving, we begin the healing process by first acknowledging or naming the abilities that we have lost. If the competence

is key to our identity—like Dr. Wallace's ability to practice medicine—the letting go may be accompanied by
powerful emotion. Letting go of a competence often carries the same pain and need to grieve as any other loss.
Unless we name our loss and mourn its passing, the abilities that had been a source of life become symbols of death.

The end of the grieving process for a lost competence
can often include a close reassessment of the wide scope
of our competencies and the ways we use them. We can
sort through those which are technical skills and those
which are human living skills. Human living skills are
always useful and can always grow. Technical skills may
be readily transferable. For example, even though Sarah
could no longer keep up with the technology of her old
job that lagging behind did not mean that she no longer
had valuable managerial skills. When Sarah let go of her
sadness and sense of inadequacy, she was able to distill
what she had learned about problem solving during her
years of management and turn that knowledge into a
private consulting practice.

Skills no longer needed in one setting may find a perfect fit in another. For instance, Dr. Wallace eventually
brought his many years of practice to the position of
medical director of a nursing home and convalescent
hospital. High technology was not the central focus of
the care of these patients. Dr. Wallace concentrated on
medicine for elders and used his wonderful skills with
patients for many years.

No one else has exactly the same knowledge and skill
and way of doing things as we do, and we can be delighted and grateful for our gifts. And, as is true of the
pattern of life, through the loss of one good—one set of

competencies—we may open ourselves to the development of other opportunities. Because we feel comfortable with what we know, however, we can fall into one of the most common traps—rigidity. Rigid attitudes rarely allow for growth. Being alive, being part of the process of the universe means always being open to change.

Reflection Exercises

◆ Relax and breathe easily and slowly. When you feel yourself becoming at ease, begin to call to mind any particular skills or abilities you have used during your life. In what ways have you been competent? Include both work competencies and human-living competencies. Writing a list of your competencies may be useful. What feedback have you received from others about your abilities? Rank your competencies as to their importance to your identity and sense of self-worth. Then ask yourself: What does my ranking tell me about myself? As I ponder my competencies, what feelings are going on inside?

◆ Examine your list of competencies or abilities, and note which of them you no longer use and, specifically, which have become outdated. Which have been the hardest to let go? What emotions or feelings emerge as you think about those you no longer use? Which do you still mourn or feel angry about? What prevents you from letting go?

◆ Focus on the loss of one diminished, lost, discarded, or outmoded skill or ability that continues to provoke hurt, sadness, or regret. Meditate and acknowledge all the ways this competence was beneficial and contributed to your life or the lives of others. Give some thought to the prestige, enjoyment, or rewards that came to you as a result of this ability. Attend to the feelings that emerge. Dialogue with Jesus about your gratitude for the ability, about the gifts it brought to you and others, and about your feelings when it was no longer needed.

◆ As you call to mind the one area in which you have felt the greatest sense of incompetence and loss, give some thought to any dimensions of those skills that you still use. How did that competence contribute to other aspects of your life? Is there anything you continue to hold on to that is asking to be released? anger? sadness? low self-esteem? blame?

◆ Could any of the lost abilities on your list be employed in other settings or in new ways? Let your imagination consider the widest range of possibilities. Ask the Holy Spirit for inspiration. If you have an understanding confidant who might have some ideas, talk with him or her about this.

◆ You may want to ritualize your letting go of a disused or lost competence. If you used to be a mail carrier, but had to retire, you might dispose of the uniform that has been gathering dust in the closet. If you can no longer play tennis, but have rackets cluttering up the house, pass them on to someone just starting. In whatever way you ritualize the letting go, include a prayer of gratitude and release. You might complete each of these sentences to form your prayer:

Gracious God, I thank you for my competence at...
Having this ability was a great gift because...
Letting go of this ability has made me feel...
To move on in life, please, God, grant me
   the grace to...

◆ Pray with God's Word. Let the meaning of the passage assist you in your grieving.

God's Word

Make me know your ways, Yahweh;
teach me your paths,
Lead me in your truth and teach me,
for you are the God of my salvation;
for you I wait all the day long.
Be mindful of your mercy, Yahweh,
and of your steadfast love.

—Psalm 25:4–6, Psalms Anew

Answer me when I call, God, my defender!
When I was in trouble, you came to my help.
Be kind to me now; hear my prayer!

—Psalm 4:1, Psalms Anew

Closing prayer: Blessed Creator, may my path and yours be the same. When any of my talents or abilities desert me or fall into disuse, let me remember that the most important competence is love. May I continually grow in love. But also, grant that I may appreciate my abilities and employ them creatively for the good of my brothers and sisters. May I always be a source of hope.

Dreams, Hopes, and Expectations

"It seems like 'someday' is never coming...."

Opening prayer: God of hope, many of my dreams and expectations have been destroyed, or at least battered. May my hope be renewed by your grace, and may I get beyond my grief at lost dreams and tarnished expectations.

Story

From early childhood, Sally dreamed of having a loving husband and a house full of children. She cherished thoughts of PTA meetings, soccer and softball games, birthday parties, and cookie baking. She envisioned parenthood through a rosy glow. Sally's dream sustained her through hard times and several unsatisfactory jobs.

Hope still burned through her early thirties. She consoled herself that she would be an even better mom with her experience in the world of work, and that someone was waiting for her just around the corner. He would be the man to match her dreams.

Sally acknowledged that life was hardly a fairy tale, so she grounded her dreams in reality. She was available. She dated, enjoyed the company of many people, and prayed to find a good, caring man.

As forty approached, deep sorrow and slow burning anger grew within Sally. Her strongest hope seemed destined to crumble. She had done everything she knew to make her life match her hopes. She wondered if she was asking too much. Other people were achieving what she wanted. Sally even asked herself if she was being punished for something. How on earth was she to proceed now, when her future lacked everything she had ever hoped for?

Commentary

We thrive on our dreams. As children, we always look forward and open many of our sentences with "When I grow up..."

We do not stop hoping, planning, and dreaming when we *are* grown up. Our expectations give direction and color to life and pull us forward with hopes for fulfillment. Sometimes we build our whole life around such dreams and plans.

Many of our dreams, especially when supported by effort and hard work, do come true. Some dreams are only partially realized. Other plans start out with great fanfare only to come crashing down around us at a later time. However, some visions are destined to remain unfulfilled no matter how hard we try. Jobs we prepared for may not materialize. A style of life we envisioned ends up being unaffordable. A circle of intimate friends gradually moves away.

We do not have to wait for midlife to feel the weight of the unmet dreams and expectations we carry around with us. The longer we live, the larger our collection becomes. Some dreams might have come true if we had worked harder, while others were unrealistic all along. The loss of our dreams also brings the loss of the other delights that may have accompanied those dreams—joy, prestige, love, excitement, and contentment. Each dream carries a whole assortment of connected delights.

Unless we stop to ponder the life and death of our dreams, an unconscious disappointment and unhappiness may hold us back from renewing dreams and making realistic plans. Indeed, we may seldom ponder our dreams, and hardly notice how much emotion is connected to them. Only when we become aware of our dreams can we begin to see the power we have given them, power that affects our life.

Unfulfilled wishes and expectations seem to give us permission to be perpetually disappointed with life, to take on the role of victim, and to live a less demanding life than we first planned. Those unmet dreams can provide us with alibis for why we are not as complete or as accomplished as we could be. We can hold on to our disappointments as ready-made reasons for shunning even attainable goals.

By grieving over lost dreams, we may evolve a more

attainable dream and more realistic plan of achieving it. At the age of eighty-one, a great-grandmother earned the college degree that lack of money and the duties of raising a family had made impossible earlier. She held on to her dream and, instead of using her frustration as an excuse, she harnessed her energies to her dream.

When dreams remain unacknowledged they tend to have much more power over us than they do when we are aware of them. If this great-grandmother had shoved her frustrated dream into the recesses of her unconscious, it would have soured, and she may never have achieved it. Acknowledging our persistent dreams may help us discover ways to live out our hopes. Unable to afford nursing school in her younger days, a woman I counseled began volunteering weekly in a hospice program. Although she never became a registered nurse, she was finally able to fulfill her desire to provide loving care for people in need.

Recognizing what has not been fulfilled for us will result in a list that offers us some choices. Within that list are those hopes we can still address if we choose. Addressing them, however, means that we can no longer bemoan what life has refused us.

Acknowledging unfulfilled hopes also brings us face to face with the hopes that will remain wholly or partially unfulfilled. We can grieve for these and, with God's grace, let go. In the letting go, we can eliminate the negative power the dreams may have in our life. We may even discover broader vistas with other realizable dreams.

The emotions that accompany the loss of hopes are usually in proportion to how much we really connect with these wishes. In fact, it is often the depth of our feeling that lets us know how important these hopes were for us. Certainly sadness is common with every lost dream. Anger may accompany our sadness because we may feel cheated out of something we thought was right-fully ours. We might be angry with someone else who prevented us from achieving our wishes—the supervisor who passed us over for a promotion, or parents who belittled our aspirations and dreams. We may feel guilt and anger toward ourself.

We accomplish nothing healthy by berating ourselves for emotion that naturally expresses the pain of our loss. Our emotions ask to be acknowledged, accepted, and released. Only then have we honored our lost dreams, and only then can we renew our hopes for the future.

Reflection Exercises

◆ After settling yourself, relax and breathe deeply and slowly. Ask for God's grace in your journey through dis-appointments and lost dreams. Call to mind the aspects of your life that seem unfulfilled. You may want to focus on one area, or bring to mind a number of unanswered prayers, wishes, or hopes. Use your journal to write down whatever comes to mind. Tune in to any anger, fear, sad-ness, or guilt, and make note of these feelings as you write. You may want to stop and let the feelings emerge. The purpose of this period of reflection is to acknowl-edge dreams deferred, plans gone awry, hopes disap-pointed. As is common, you may also uncap a well of emotion.

◆ When you have acknowledged lost dreams, review the list and then write next to each one any other losses connected to the dream. For instance, Sally, whose story was told at the beginning of this chapter, could tie other things to her dream of being a mother: involvement with other parents and establishing a solid role in her community. While some dreams, though intense, may not be quite this encompassing, all dreams have related benefits that are also lost. Try to get in touch with these.

◆ Pick one item from your list of unfulfilled hopes about which you feel sorrow or loss most keenly. Draw or find a picture of this expectation or hope. As you draw or ponder the picture, become aware of feelings that arise. Welcome the feelings, even if they are uncomfortable. Recognize them as ways of expressing what the dream meant to you. If you want to cry, cry. If you feel a song rising from the feelings, sing. If you feel angry, be angry. Tear up the drawing or picture, or burn it in your anger. Realize that release from grief takes time—ask for God's grace so that you may fully let go.

You may need to repeat this exercise for this or other unfulfilled dreams.

◆ When you feel free of the strongest emotion, pray these words: "God, I release this dream, or hope...into your hands. I am thankful for the delight it brought me, for letting go of it, and for all the pain of its loss. I value myself as a hoping person, full of expectations of good things in my life."

◆ Ponder these questions and do some journal writing about them: What do I want to change in my life as I let go of the unfulfilled dreams? (For instance, you may need to stop complaining about how life has not been fair. Or perhaps you need to do an assessment of alternate means of fulfilling a dream.) What graces do I need from God to change my life?

◆ Finally, list some hopes and dreams that are still possible and attractive. Identify some new hopes and dreams that can give you energy to move forward at this point in your life, now that you are letting go of the old dreams. Ask for guidance and strength from the Holy Spirit.

◆ Pray with God's Word. Let the meaning of the passage aid you in your grieving.

God's Word

> *For in hope we were saved. Now hope that is seen is not hope. For who hopes for what is seen? But if we hope for what we do not see, we wait for it with patience.... We know that all things work to-gether for good for those who love God.*
>
> —*Romans 8:24–28*, NRSV

Closing prayer: God of dreams, hopes, and expectations, you prepare wondrous things for us. Accept all my un-fulfilled dreams, which are shadows of my desire for you. I release them to you. I let them go freely, along with all the pain and sadness of their loss. Take them and trans-form them into my fulfillment and growth in you.

Status or "Face"

"I'm so embarrassed...."

Opening prayer: God, I find so many things to be embarrassed about, so many ways to lose face. You know and love my real face. Help me to let go of all the false faces and images that I like to hide behind, and come to see that each person—me included—is "number one" with you. Teach me true humility, which is living honestly with the knowledge that without you, I am nothing.

Story

From the age of ten, Brian knew he would be a lawyer. His playmates frequently wound up in his imaginary courtroom, designated as judges, witnesses, plaintiffs, and defendants. He played other games only rarely. In every assigned school essay that allowed a choice of topic, Brian wrote about some aspect of being a lawyer. He thought that being a lawyer was the best thing anyone could be.

Nothing about high school distracted Brian from his goal. He joined the debate team and took writing and speech classes. He judiciously applied to a select group of colleges with good prelaw courses.

In college Brian studied diligently, though a superior grade point average eluded him. He joined the prelaw club and developed an interest in many causes. Brian planned to make his mark in the realm of social change. By now, family, friends, teachers, classmates, relatives, and even acquaintances knew of his plans and hopes. When he daydreamed of himself as an attorney, he swelled with pride.

Brian asked the most influential people he knew to write letters of recommendation for law schools. He felt sure that he would have his choice of the schools he applied to. At his college graduation, Brian received gifts that any eager law student would need.

When the first letter of rejection arrived, Brian could not believe it. Quickly he reasoned that it was tough to get in to law school, and with so many applicants it only made sense that one of the schools would say no. He breathed a bit easier and waited to see which school would be the one to open its arms to him.

When the second letter began, "We are sorry to inform you...," Brian was dumbfounded. How could this be? There was only one more possibility. What if that didn't work out? What would he do? What would he say now to everybody? How could he explain that two schools had refused him? How embarrassing!

The final rejection was devastating. Convinced that a mistake had been made, Brian called the school to be sure the letter was accurate. The curt voice on the other end of the line said, "No, there's no mistake. You were not admitted."

His hopes collapsed. And he suddenly wondered what people would think. For years, he had been talking as if he were already a lawyer. "I'm so embarrassed!" he confided to his mother.

In his humiliation, Brian hid from people and, much to his further shame, found himself crying uncontrollably. He wondered what he had done wrong to be punished like this. Brian swore that God had abandoned him. He had made no plans for anything else. He could not even imagine anything else.

Then it dawned on Brian that the whole world saw him as a failure. His friends, his family, everyone he knew—classmates, friends of friends, even his father's coworkers—all of them now knew that he did not make it, that he was not good enough, that he had failed. Brian was not sure how he would ever face anybody again.

Commentary

In response to what we believe the external world expects of us, we create an image of ourselves to show to other people. This image, or face, corresponds to what we want others to believe we are and carries with it rewards of respect and approval. Frequently, the image we cultivate becomes a mask, covering up our real self. Brian acted like he thought lawyers act. Executives tend to assume the image that society thinks managers should have.

Our culture grants a certain status to each profession. For better or worse, professors have been given more status than elementary teachers, doctors more than nurses. Most jobs have a particular status with all the attendant adulation and expectations. We easily become wedded to our status because it gives us a sense of self-worth.

Most of us work hard to preserve our image, closing our eyes to the fact that it is only a mask or a role. Often we believe that the image *is* who we are, because the image is how we *wish* to be perceived and evaluated in this world—how we want others to see us, and what we want them to believe about us.

From Asian culture we have learned the expression "losing face." Losing face means that our image has been destroyed by our failure, our humiliation, or by our misdeeds. To lose face carries the connotation of a loss of dignity, of self-respect, and of prestige—enormous losses. We seek face-saving solutions to dilemmas so that everyone involved will not be embarrassed or exposed.

In life, few of us escape for long without some experience of loss of face. Some of these experiences are tiny and some are shattering. Each embarrassment damages our self-image. We lose some sense of ourself as proper, worthy, or appropriate. The more we are attached to the image that our faux pas attacks, the greater the loss for us.

We strive to maintain the illusion we have created, but this self-image usually begins to crumble over time. In our search for personal growth and healthy development, we become increasingly aware of the masks we wear. We begin to let go of false images and learn to accept ourselves as we truly are. Allowing greater consciousness about ourselves changes the balance of power in our life, because as long as any aspect of ourselves remains unconscious, it can control and affect us in ways we may not notice.

With greater self-awareness, we can make efforts to change some of what we do not like. A young woman I knew felt embarrassed about her fractured grammar. Because she is aware of the problem, she now works hard to speak more effectively. On the other hand, Joe, a personnel manager, denied his racial prejudices to himself and to others. When he was brought up on charges of discrimination, he was thunderstruck. Although Joe had never hired a minority applicant, he also never considered himself a bigot.

Striving for self-knowledge and self-acceptance makes sense, but we will still at times lose face and experience humiliation. When we do make a mistake or experience a loss of face, our response may naturally be embarrassment and distress. We begin our grieving and recovery by acknowledging just what it was that we lost in a particular instance. Once we know what has been lost, we can decide its value for us and whether we want to hold such a value.

Brian, in our opening scenario, saw becoming a lawyer as his lifelong primary value. When life—in the guise of three law schools—took away that choice, Brian naturally reacted with great distress. Once he made his way through his pain and sadness, Brian had some choices to make. Was his worth as a person dependent upon his being a lawyer? Did the law schools' decisions mean that Brian was completely incompetent and of no value? Did he truly let his family and friends down? What would really happen when he faced them all again? Did he want to let people's judgments ruin his life? What might be gained by these rejections? Where could he choose to go from here?

Loss of face or status will never be easy. It should be grieved, but like all losses, it offers us opportunities for growth if we do not let the loss hang on and gnaw at our soul.

Reflection Exercises

◆ Call to mind the fact that you are already in the presence of God, who loves you as you are and with whom you need have no embarrassment. Relax in that presence. Gradually begin to note the times when you lost face, instances that continue to arouse emotion in you. Notice also those losses that no longer upset you. What is it that makes these losses different? Did you handle them differently?

◆ As you remember the losses of prestige or the times of rejection or embarrassment, try to discover what it was that you lost in each experience. Is there still need to grieve over those losses?

◆ When you have been embarrassed throughout your life, is there any common experience that you find provokes that reaction? What do you most dread: looking "dumb"? being clumsy? not winning? Is there anything you can learn about yourself that you may want to let go of and grieve over? Ask for God's grace to explore these questions.

◆ If you still smart from a humiliation at someone's hands, acknowledge that moment. Who was there? What happened? When did it occur? Where were you? Why did it take place? What are your feelings right now? Ask the Holy Spirit dwelling within you what you can do to let go of the loss of face and for the grace to let go.

◆ After you move through memories of embarrassing moments and feel all the emotions associated with them, use this prayer or a similar one: "Merciful Creator, I give to you all my embarrassing moments, and all the feelings that go with them. Please take them and transform them into the grace of self-love and understanding. Remind me that I'm not perfect, and that you love me as I am and love my efforts to move through my embarrassments."

◆ Pray with the Word of God, and let its meaning assist you in your grieving.

God's Word

> God will cleanse every tear
> from our face and remove all our shame.
>
> —*Adapted from Isaiah 25:8*

> Yahweh, you search me and know me.
> You know if I am standing or sitting.
> You perceive my thoughts from far away.
> Whether I walk or lie down, you are watching;
> you are familiar with all my ways.
>
> —*Psalm 139:1–3*, Psalms Anew

You created my inmost being
and knit me together in my mother's womb.
For all these mysteries—
for the wonder of myself,
for the wonder of your works—
I thank you.

—*Psalm 139:13–14,* Psalms Anew

Closing prayer: Saving God, you know us exactly as we are and love us anyway. Help me to put aside my masks and see myself as you see me—as someone lovable. Show me that my imperfections can be the very vehicles for my journey toward wholeness in you. Strengthen my ability to see myself as I truly am, and to use that perception as the beginning of my growth.

Integrity and Self-Respect

"I'll never be worth anything again...."

Opening prayer: God of hope, you made us "a little less than the angels," and you gave us the gift of free will. Be with me as I struggle with some of my bad choices. Help me to make them happy faults that lead me back to your mercy, your wisdom, your love. Through my repentance and grieving, may I be graced with the integrity and self-love that you want for all your people.

Story

A long time passed before Anne could tell anybody about what she had done. Even admitting it to herself proved a struggle. Finally, she had to make things right.

First, she had anonymously paid the full amount to the store. Now she was tearfully confessing to her best friend, "I don't know what came over me, but when I was trying on gold bracelets, the clerk was called to the other side of the counter. It happened so fast, I couldn't believe I'd done it! I just slipped one of the bracelets into my purse. There were enough of them out that I knew she'd never know one was gone. And once I'd done it there was no way I could undo it, because she'd know! So I just thanked her, said I wanted to wait and look around, and got out of the store as fast as I could."

Anne had spent four months carrying her secret. Immediately after snatching the bracelet, Anne felt a mixture of relief and guilt: relief at not being caught, guilt about stealing. She hid the bracelet away in the bottom of her chest of drawers, thinking that she would figure out a way to slip it into the store's showcase without anyone's knowledge. Eventually, Anne sent cash to the store with a typed note that it was for something taken.

Even making restitution did not ease Anne's guilt. She could not bring herself to wear the bracelet. It had come to symbolize something awful to her. "I'm a thief," Anne sobbed to her friend. "I must be a terrible person. I've never stolen anything before. But I must have wanted to, or I wouldn't have taken this so quickly, as soon as I had a chance."

Barbara, her friend, came over and put her arm around Anne, saying, "Annie, you're my best friend! You've done so many good things for me and for other people. Of course you're not a terrible person." Barbara asked Anne what else she needed to do, considering that she had already paid the full value of the bracelet to the store.

"I went to confession, but I still feel so guilty. I'm not sure I can trust myself anymore. Every time I go shopping now, I'm a nervous wreck, afraid I won't be able to control myself. I don't even want to go to the same store for fear they'll know and be waiting for me. If I can't even trust myself, how can you or anybody else trust me? I'll never be worth anything."

Commentary

Along with our ability to do good, we all have a comparable capacity to do evil. We can be enormously loving, kind, and generous, and we also can be hateful, destructive, and stingy. Inevitably we fail, and when we do, our integrity and self-respect take a beating.

Because we hate to see evil in ourselves, we are often tempted to deny our sinfulness. We may exonerate ourselves from responsibility with a thousand clever excuses. However, if our conscience is alive and well, even if it is buried deeply under our rationalizations, it will goad us to acknowledge our wrongdoing. In the best case, our discomfort over failure pulls us to admit, repent, and learn from it.

Our sin needs to be grieved because we have lost our integrity. Through our failings, we lose the belief in ourselves as good, trustworthy, and kind—persons created in the image of God. The grace-filled grieving of our sinfulness follows the same pattern as that of other experiences of loss. First, we acknowledge the loss, like Anne did when she sent in the money and told her friend. If we genuinely feel the loss, we can be cleansed by the flood of sorrow and guilt. In fact, the emotions we feel— embarrassment, shame, emptiness, and so on—tell us what we value and push us to think about what we have done and what we might learn from the experience.

In grieving our loss of integrity, the most difficult

movement might be the last one, choosing to change the things we do that keep us tied to our sense of lost self-respect or even to the evil behavior.

When we have failed, we may become tied to our guilt or lost self-esteem. A painful example of this was Sandra. She was an excellent nurse—perceptive, competent, and genuinely concerned about her patients. In the midst of a very busy day, Sandra administered a slight overdose of medication to a patient who had a severe reaction to the dosage. Though Sandra's mistake was serious, the patient survived and even reassured and forgave Sandra. Despite years of patient care unblemished by error, Sandra would not allow herself to move beyond this mistake. She resigned and left nursing. Her colleagues, the nursing supervisor, and the doctors tried to persuade Sandra that some error is unavoidable and that she should continue, but Sandra would not hear them. Not only did Sandra deprive herself of an opportunity to grow through this crisis, she deprived many patients of the wonderful care that she could have given them.

One part of changing things in our grief over lost integrity and self-respect is choosing to let go of our guilt. When we are willing to acknowledge our failings and move through them, we have the opportunity to become more sensitive, stronger, more attentive, and so on. Aware of her own imperfection, Sandra might have discovered new compassion for her patients. Sandra, the wounded healer, might have been even more effective than Sandra the perfect nurse.

Anne's shoplifting experience may force her to look at her attachment to material things. Her guilt and loss of self-respect invite her to reexamine her focus on possessions. If Anne uses her guilt as a steppingstone for learning and growth, the loss becomes a "happy fault" that leads to conversion.

Besides letting go of our guilt, another way we move through healthy grieving is by making a firm decision to alter our harmful behavior. If we change the behavior with God's grace, we avoid repeating the deed and regretting it over and over. Unless our failing, grieving, and repenting bring us to this step, we have not completed the process. When we refuse to accept the grace of conversion and complete the process, we may hold on to self-defeating and destructive patterns. By a refusal to move through our failings, we doom ourselves to live under the pall of lost integrity.

Reflection Exercises

◆ Sit quietly, take some deep breaths, and relax. Remind yourself that you are in the presence of God, in God's hands, being held with the greatest of love. Bring to mind whatever failings or wrongs you may have done that are still asking for your attention. Some may be very obvious and recent, some may be buried from long ago. Simply name them, and be aware of the feelings that come along with them. You may want to write in your journal about the thoughts and feelings that come.

◆ Take one particular failing of which you are keenly aware, and ponder what other losses may be associated with it. Have you changed the way you see yourself or feel about yourself as a result of it? Have you changed the way you do things as a result of the failing? Again, there may be feelings that come up with each loss you find. Just let the emotions arise.

◆ Ponder a failing you may be struggling with, and consider what it may be able to teach you. How can you grow as a result of that failing? How is the failing calling you to live differently? Talk with the Holy Spirit about this.

◆ With any failing you recall, give some thought to what you still need to do with it or about it. For your examination of conscience, pose these questions to yourself about each cause of lost self-respect:

❖ When I recall this failing, what feelings do I have? What do they tell me about my need for repentance or grieving?
❖ Do I keep repeating this action? Why? Do I honestly want to change my ways?
❖ What graces do I need from God to live rightly and avoid this failing?
❖ What action do I need to take to live uprightly and turn this failing into a happy fault?

Ask for God's grace to turn your life around and to let go of the loss of self-respect.

◆ Are you aware of any clinging to past failings, or to feelings about yourself because of the failings? What are you getting out of holding on to these past failings and the attendant emotions?

◆ When you identify any failings that have been especially difficult for you to accept or acknowledge, or any feelings about yourself that are despairing, talk to Christ about it and ask for specific help. You may want to use this prayer, or frame your own: "O God, here are some really tough things for me to admit....I want to make my way through them, but I'm having a terrible time. Let me see that each little step I take in getting through them is a step toward my personal growth and my closeness to you. Help me to know that I don't have to keep feeling bad about myself."

◆ Pray God's Word. Let it console and challenge you to grieve for the lost self-respect and to turn your life toward God.

God's Word

Bless Yahweh, O my soul.
Bless God's holy name, all that is in me!
Bless Yahweh, O my soul,
and remember God's faithfulness:
in forgiving all my offenses,
in healing all my diseases,
in redeeming my life from destruction,
in crowning me with love and compassion.

—*Psalm 103:1–4*, Psalms Anew

Neither death, nor life, nor angels, nor rulers, nor things present, nor things to come, nor powers, nor height, nor depth, nor anything else in all creation, will be able to separate us from the love of God in Christ Jesus.

—Romans 8:38–39, NRSV

Closing prayer: God of forgiveness and healing, I turn my faults and failings over to you, with all of the bad feelings they have engendered in me. Wipe out my offenses, and pull me out of the pit of my distress. May I grow strong and whole in you, and may I continue to say yes to constant renewal. Help me to value myself as a unique manifestation of you and to act accordingly.

A Companion Animal

"It was only a dog...."

Opening prayer: God our Creator, you show yourself in all of your creatures. Thank you for the gift of our animal companions, whose presence enriches us. Help me in my sadness and grief over the loss of my companion.

Story

Marko, Joan's big boxer, took up residence under Joan's desk when she worked, followed her from room to room, stretched out on the rug in front of the sink while she did dishes. He slept in her bedroom and accompanied her on errands in the car, his boxer muzzle sticking out the window, lapping up the air.

Until Marko, Joan had been scared of dogs. In fact, she had to struggle with herself to consent to his arrival. Her sister raved about how beautiful Marko was and reminded Joan that she had always said she would not be afraid if she "could only have a baby boxer who could grow up with me."

So Marko came bounding into Joan's life and proceeded to show her life through a dog's eyes, teaching her all kinds of things she did not know. His exuberance for life rubbed off on Joan. In the mornings, even before she was fully awake, Marko's delighted leaping around the backyard made her laugh. Right on time, twice a day, his slobbering, enthusiastic anticipation of being fed never failed to bring a smile to her face. He greeted the same old dog chow like Thanksgiving dinner guests "oohing" and "aahing" over a perfectly browned turkey and sage-fragrant dressing. A simple walk around the neighborhood became an adventure of sniffing, licking, and spying discovery.

While Marko had favorite people and animals, he could make even generally grumpy people act friendly. He just knew that people were glad to see him, and he would sometimes throw his big body against them in his excitement. He accepted others for who they were.

In what seemed the twinkling of an eye, Marko grew old. Cancer began to consume his huge vitality. Joan could not believe it. She sought any treatment that promised to restore Marko to health. Losing this animal companion was unthinkable; he had become a comforting, lively, and essential part of her world. Nevertheless, as the cancer spread throughout his body, Joan painfully admitted that she would have to let him go. The sight of his pain-dulled eyes and crippled walk overwhelmed her desire to hold on to his life. She never knew how hard such a decision could be, and how much grief could accompany the loss of an animal friend.

Commentary

Human beings often develop companion relationships with animals. The reasons vary, but the fact that we tend to bond with animals is indisputable. When a significant connection exists between a person and an animal, coping with the loss of this special creature follows the same movements as all grieving.

However, people who are grieving the loss of an animal companion sometimes encounter others who attempt to minimize the loss. In stumbling attempts to console us, people say things like "Don't feel so bad. It was just a cat!" or "Just forget about it; it was only a dog," or "You can always get another one!" These kinds of statements belittle and negate our pain and sorrow, and they certainly do not eliminate our need to grieve the death of our animal friend. We must give ourself permission to grieve. We have lost a significant part of ourself.

Anyone who has bonded with a pet knows that animals, like people, are unique individuals. No two Dalmatians, no two Siamese cats, are alike. Each has a unique temperament and personality, and each approaches life with an individual style. Because no pet can replace another, every relationship with a companion animal is special.

We experience varying degrees of connecting with animals. Some dog owners may view their animal as a source of protection that stays out in the yard. Their bonding would probably be less intense than that of the housebound person, whose dog may be the only other living and responding being in the home. A cat can be charming and diverting. "Whenever I felt down," Judy said,

"Bingo was there to lift my spirits. She was great to have around." For other cat owners, the relationship can be deeper. While grieving over his cat's death, Mark said, "That cat really took me out of myself and forced me to think of something besides myself. Having him around and taking care of him was the greatest decision I ever made. It really changed me as a person."

A relationship with a companion animal may have many more components than we realize. A dog or cat may provide not only pleasant company but also the nonjudgmental acceptance that is all too rarely given by human companions. A relationship with a pet can open us to the world in ways no human relationship can. Imagining the world through the eyes and ears of a dog or cat sharpens our perceptive ability. Animals can teach us to live in the present and to appreciate the smallest of gifts. Opening up to animal wisdom can stretch us and push us toward growth. Studies conducted in hospitals and nursing homes have demonstrated that relationships with animals can be healing.

When a companion animal dies, we may find ourselves floundering in unexpected grief. For the first time, we may have to recognize the strong bond with the animal. Not only do we lose a pet, but we also lose other intangible gifts. For instance, if a cat was a gift from someone significant who has since gone out of our life, the cat's death may trigger unresolved grief from the other loss.

Our emotions over the death of a pet may give us some indication of what our losses are. "Not only was I sad after Sundance died," Maria said, "I really felt angry about it. The more I thought about my anger, the more I could see that I felt so helpless. With Sundance, it was the first time in my life I had any control over anything. He was my dog, and I took good care of him, and nobody could tell me what to do with him. I made the decisions. And now he's gone."

We may feel deeply needed because a pet is so dependent on us. Caring for a cat or dog calls us to be protective and responsible. So when a pet dies, we may blame ourself for failing in our care. Many times we could not have changed anything. Sometimes we may indeed be at fault. In counseling, Julie sobbed aloud as she told of being ordered by the courts to euthanize her dog after a number of incidents of biting. "It was all my fault that he had to die," she cried. "I thought he was so cute as a puppy when he'd nip at me, I never made him stop. And then later I couldn't." Whether we are blameless or not, the death of our animal friend strikes deeply.

Deciding to euthanize a companion animal may tie our insides in knots. In fact, many people find this decision harder than the actual death of the animal. Long afterward, they find themselves wondering if they could have done more. Guilt may mix with other emotions even when we know that the decision was a loving one.

To move beyond our grief, we must bring to our awareness all that we lost with the death of our pet and let the emotions flow. Then we can make decisions about how to move on. It is important, as in any other loss, not to "fill in the spot" too quickly. We should not expect a new pet to erase the need for our grief. Not grieving would be doing ourself a disservice. Certainly, we may eventually want to bring a new creature into our life. However, allowing some time for grieving is an important gift to ourself. We have lost a unique, irreplaceable manifestation of God in creation. The loss deserves our respect and our grief.

Reflection Exercises

◆ Sit comfortably, take some slow and deep breaths, and relax. Bring to mind any companion animals you have lost through the course of your life. List their names in your journal. If you have pictures of these pets, find and look at them. Consider the uniqueness of each pet and what made each relationship special. Describe each pet and tell God what you loved about each one. Note what you learned in each relationship. Remember that you are in God's presence as you ponder the memories of these pets. Stay in touch with your feelings. Is there any unfinished grief over the loss of a particular pet?

◆ Call to mind one particular pet whose loss still brings pain and sorrow. Think about the components of your relationship with this pet. What else did you lose when you lost this animal? How do you feel right now when you think of him or her? What do these emotions tell you about the significance of your relationship?

Picture that pet on the lap or at the side of Jesus. Talk to them both about your feelings. When you finish, entrust that special pet to Jesus' care.

◆ Give some thought to the lessons you have learned through relationships with your pets. What wisdom did they bring? How are they still alive in you now through their wisdom?

◆ Are you a better person as a result of your relationships with your companion animals? more caring? more
sensitive? more perceptive?

◆ Pray with God's Word. Let the meaning of the passages assist you in your grieving and in your awareness
of the relationship with your pet.

God's Word

> *But ask the animals, and they will teach you;*
> *the birds of the air, and they will tell you;*
> *ask the plants of the earth, and they will teach you;*
> *and the fish of the sea will declare to you.*
> *Who among all these does not know*
> *that the hand of [God] has done this?*
> *In [God's] hand is the life of every living thing….*
>
> —*Job 12:7–40*, NRSV

> *Yahweh is generous to all,*
> *[God's] tenderness embraces all…creatures.*
>
> —*Psalm 145:9*, NJB

Closing prayer: Tender Creator, you manifest yourself
in every creature and in every part of your universe. Show
me that when my heart is not open to these creatures, I
am in danger of missing your exuberance and playful-
ness, your charm and outright love for me. Grant me the
grace to be a care-filled steward of your creatures, large
and small. I thank you especially for …. Now free me
from my grief over the death of ….

REFLECTION 12

Confidence in Religious Beliefs

"It isn't the same church it used to be...."

Opening prayer: Living God, help me face the challenges to my beliefs with confidence in you. As I let go of the faith of my childhood to gain a belief that will sustain me now, lead me through my grief to learn, grow, and come closer to you. Be with me now as I search for wholeness and healing.

Story

Dan grumbled angrily when he left church after Sunday Mass. "I don't even feel like I went to Mass," he complained to his wife, Barbara, as they drove off. "I get so upset by the way they're doing things I can't even pray! What's the point of going anymore?"

Barbara had tried to reason with Dan before, but he

87

had just blown up at her. She did not like the way things had changed at church anymore than Dan did, but she felt disloyal if she did not defend the Church. She didn't understand the changes either.

Dan and Barbara were "cradle Catholics," products of elementary and secondary Catholic education. They had studied the catechism and believed one of the best things about their faith was that it would always be the same—they knew exactly where they stood. They had been taught to defend everything about the Church and its beliefs.

Their staunch set of beliefs and practices gave Dan and Barbara comfort. Dan argued, "Isn't that what religion is all about?" No matter where in the whole world they went to Mass, it was the same. "It was something you could count on," Dan explained. "You never worried about what to believe—you just knew. You didn't even have to think about it! I felt secure."

Now everything about the Church seemed to be in turmoil. Some churches had altars in the center, and some were moved out from the wall and turned around. When the Latin went, the mystery was gone. Guitars, flutes, and even tambourines were used now, and new songs displaced old favorites. Dan refused to sing with any guitar in church. Even though he was friendly, Dan disliked having to shake hands with people he did not even know. He had been taught to protect his faith, but now it seemed the biggest attack on it came from the people running the church! Dan kept going to church, but would go to the back where he could follow along with his Latin missal and block out as much as he could around him.

Dan had been thrown further into turmoil when

priests and religious began leaving their communities. He could not understand such lack of commitment. It irritated him to no end when the sisters turned the grade schools over to laypeople, even though he complained to Barbara that "you couldn't even tell who the sisters were without their traditional habits."

Finally, Dan's confidence in the Church received a staggering blow. In the last three weeks, two priests in the diocese had been charged with sexual abuse of teenagers. As he read the stories, his stomach turned. A dark cloud of doubt spread its gloom over Dan. Questions that he had never considered began to knock at his consciousness: "Have I been wrong all these years? Has God abandoned the Church? Has it all been for nothing?" Amid this crisis, Dan continued to go to church, but he felt as if somebody had died.

Commentary

Change is a sign of life. Winter flows into spring. Eggs hatch into eagles. Babies become stalwart adults.

Even so, people keep searching for something permanent and immutable to hold on to. We sense that we can better handle change when we have steady footing. The story of a healthy life seems to be the constant balancing of these two forces—security and holding on, or letting go and changing. Fullness of life exists when these forces dance together in harmony—sometimes one leading, and sometimes the other. If we are not moving, we are not dancing. If we move erratically, or faster than the music, we are not dancing. God is, as the old Shaker song proclaims, "Lord of the Dance." God invites us to dance.

Grasping at security, refusing all change, and living in ruts can be deadly. The only difference between a rut and a grave is the depth. It can be equally harmful, however, to have no grounding, no solid beliefs in our life. When we move with every wind that blows, we may have no sense of who we are. A popular country music song reflects just such a problem, "You've got to stand for something or you'll fall for anything!"

For many of us, religious beliefs provide the most solid footing that we have. God is our rock, our fortress, our stronghold. The knowledge that God never changes gives us some comfort in the midst of turmoil, trouble, and uncertainty.

From our belief in God as supremely stable, it is easy to accept the notion that anything to do with God will have the same stability. For many of us, this belief was reinforced by our experience. For many years, nothing seemed to change in the Church. Religious practices went unquestioned. We came to believe that immutability was the nature of religion.

Change can make us feel insecure and also calls into question all that we previously relied on. We feel that we have no sure footing, and we worry whether we will be able to cope with something different. When we believe that what is changing has to do with our eternal security, another factor comes into play—fear. Because we often identify our faith with its expression, any sign of change in the expression can pose a threat.

We often ignore the fact that when we are off balance from the loss of religious tradition, new life can come about. Religion is living and growing. While our core beliefs may not change, the ways in which we understand

and express them may develop throughout our life. In his epistle to the Hebrews (5:12–14), Paul talks of our need to move beyond milk and get to solid food, to continue to grow in our understanding. Indeed, maturation in faith demands change. God never changes, and yet God is ever new. God is inexhaustible, infinite, and always beyond our expectations and imaginings. Paul tells the Romans: "O the depth of the riches and wisdom and knowledge of God! How unsearchable are [God's] judgments and how inscrutable [God's] ways" (11:33, NRSV). Even the central command of Jesus leaves much for us to discern. After all, the Bible does not tell us *how* to love our neighbor or love God in specific detail. No matter how unsettling for us, we always have more to experience about God. If God were immediately understandable, if we could quickly plumb the depths of God's way, God would not be God. We want stability, clear answers, and precise definitions, but that is not God's way.

Therefore, when we feel lost, when our doubts about religion multiply, when our confidence is shaken, God is often inviting us to look into our beliefs more deeply. God asks us to rely more on the Holy Spirit and less on our reason or will, to let go of pat answers and plunge into the mystery of God.

The challenge to religious people is to be open to God. Some of our religious practices may remain helpful in leading us to God, some may need to be challenged and changed. We need to seek a balance here: life offers comfort and challenge, settling down and change.

Changes wrought in the Church may be one cause of confusion and loss, but scandals from leaders of the

Church also cause us to lose confidence in the Church and cast a dark shadow on our belief. Since we expect the Church to act as it believes, instances of abuse or malfeasance rock our security about institutions composed of human beings—fallible, sinful, competent, charitable human beings like us. Again, our sense of loss needs to be named and grieved. Such a crisis also invites us to fix our faith more firmly on Christ, to sort out what is central to our faith and what is superfluous.

The emotions that arise as we think about our losses in religious beliefs may help us in several ways. Emotions can move our grieving along and can also give us clues about what our losses actually might be. For example, feeling forlorn and helpless may indicate that our losses have a lot to do with security concerns. Feeling angry toward authority figures may indicate an over-reliance on something or someone that was lost. We are forced to look at ourselves anew and call on God's grace.

As painful as the dying to old beliefs and practices may be, God is beckoning for us to take ownership of our faith, to weigh our commitments, and to make a leap of new faith. In this way, our relationship with God is in our hands.

Reflection Exercises

◆ After settling yourself comfortably, take some deep breaths and relax. Call to mind anything pertaining to your experience with church or religion that has been upsetting to you. Write in your journal the specifics of these distresses. Make some attempt to know clearly what you feel you have lost. Be sure to note the feelings that accompany each of these areas. Are they different for each or all the same? Do you see any common features?

◆ If one change or challenge to your faith has particularly bothered you, bring that area to mind. Then use these questions to guide your meditation:

❖ What loss is involved?
❖ Was it comfort you lost—a feeling of closeness to God, a feeling of closeness to your parents who taught you what to believe, or a feeling of knowing what to expect and how to act?
❖ Was it a sense of security that you lost—that as long as you did certain things certain ways, you had a sort of "life insurance" or even "death insurance"?
❖ Did your belief or practice make you feel special? If so, how? Is this lost now?
❖ Did you lose trust in religious authorities?

Remember that your sense of loss may have elements of all these factors.

◆ Have you let go of something you need to hold on to? Are you holding on to something you need to release? How can your distress over loss become the foundation or stimulus for growth? What do you need to do differently? What graces do you need from God to make needed changes?

◆ When you ponder the loss of confidence in your religious beliefs, are any fears associated with that distress?

◆ What is the fear connected to? If you find fear, say this prayer: "O God, who said love casts out fear, I know that I'm afraid of.... I trust you and love you and know that your love can remove my fear. I turn it over to you and ask that you help me move along in confidence."

◆ Ponder what it means for God to be ever ancient and ever new. In what ways can that apply to your present concerns about the changes and challenges of your faith?

◆ When we are under stress, we have three basic options: to *change* the situation, to *get out* of the situation, or to *change our attitude* about the situation. Given your sense of loss about your religious commitments or beliefs, to which of these three options are you being called? Pray that the Holy Spirit will guide you in your discernment.

◆ Dialogue with God about whether changes in religious practices have affected your relationship.

◆ Meditate on God's Word below. What do James's words tell you about your own situation in regard to your faith?

God's Word

Try to treat the trials to your faith as a happy privilege; you understand that your faith is only put to the test to make you patient, but patience too is to have its practical results so that you will become fully developed, complete, with nothing missing.

—Adapted from James 1:2–4

Closing prayer: Living God, infinite yet always new, help me to hold on to what is essential, and to be open to changing what will help me grow in faith, hope, and love. May I ever be mindful of your holy presence underlying everything.

REFLECTION 13

Health

❦

"Is life worth living like this?..."

Opening prayer: God of healing, you created us to be fully alive. Help me to find wholeness of body, mind, and spirit. And when I am ill and weak, show me how my suffering can be a steppingstone to you.

Story

Bridget thought that she had just twisted her leg sliding into second base. There was no pain, but she did feel some weakness. She ignored it and helped her company team keep winning. She loved the involvement and activity. In fact, when softball season ended, she poured her energy into volunteer coaching for the local high school volleyball team. Life was good when Bridget could balance her job as an assistant accounting supervisor with lots of physical activity.

At thirty-four, Bridget felt strong and healthy. Infrequent

colds and flu only emphasized her appreciation of being healthy and active. So when the weakness in her leg persisted, Bridget was surprised. After several weeks, Bridget determined that she probably just needed therapy for a pulled muscle or whatever.

Her doctor's concern puzzled Bridget. He ordered a batch of tests that made Bridget increasingly anxious. Two weeks dragged by. When she walked into the doctor's office to hear the results, her usual brisk confidence had evaporated.

"Bridget, it looks like you have the beginnings of multiple sclerosis." She sat in shock, knowing that some mistake had been made.

Over the next weeks, Bridget saw several specialists, hoping that someone would tell her it was not true. Not only was the diagnosis confirmed, but more symptoms started to appear. Within months she had to depend on a walker. Her physical therapist tried to prepare her for using a wheelchair. Bridget's emotions fluctuated between calm and desperation, anger and hope.

Bridget's days as an athlete had come to a screeching halt. Work took Herculean effort and some assistance from her colleagues. Gradually, she spent increasing time in bed. She needed help with even routine matters. Within one year, Bridget's entire life had turned upside down.

Sadness and anger nearly overwhelmed her. Many days Bridget felt the chill of despair. She struggled to make some sense of what seemed a worthless existence and wondered if God was punishing her for something. She found herself tripping over the questions: Why? Why did this happen to me? Why should I go on living?

Commentary

All illnesses, whether temporary, chronic, or terminal, bring losses with them. All affect our sense of self and our emotions. Each illness carries unique meanings for the sufferer, as well as implications for the future. Gerald, a robust university professor of psychology, suffered a heart attack, but his consequent insecurity was almost worse. Even though his cardiologist gave a positive prognosis, Gerald felt that the attack had robbed him of something important. He declared, "Never again will I have the sense of wholeness and freedom I had before this hit. From here on, I'm a person who's had a heart attack, and that will always be on my mind"

The meanings we attach to our losses vary vastly. After a hysterectomy, one woman may be relieved at having a problem solved, one may grieve over the loss of her ability to bear children, and one may feel that she has lost her femininity and attractiveness. While the objective losses are the same, each of us grieves over our own unique and subjective loss.

Many illnesses presage other losses to come. Chronic illness, as in Bridget's case, may begin a whole series of losses. Not only did Bridget lose a sense of well-being, she lost the use of parts of her body, her job, her independence, her sense of self-esteem, and even her desire to live.

Any kind of illness—great and sustained or minimal and passing—is an experience of loss and hints at the most dramatic loss of all—death. Even when our illness or injury is not very serious, a niggling sense that "I could die from this" scratches at our awareness. Awareness of the fragility of our very humanity nearly always brings anxiety. Because we tend to find intimations of our demise frightening, we tend to go to great lengths to squash them.

Refusing to acknowledge our vulnerability may do great harm. Jane discovered in her forties that she had developed diabetes. Distraught by the demands of her condition, she simply continued on as if it were not so. Only after she was found near death in a diabetic coma did she come to realize that her life depended on acknowledging her diabetes and following a strict regimen of care. To ignore the ways illness affects us may undermine our very efforts to cope.

Once we have acknowledged the losses we are experiencing, emotion tends to well up in us. Sadness, anger, frustration, depression, guilt, and fear may invade us. We may become resentful of the good health of others. And sometimes despair may scourge us with desperate thoughts. About her long suffering from tuberculosis, Saint Thérèse of Lisieux admitted, "If I had not had any faith, I would have committed suicide without an instant's hesitation" (John Clarke, *St. Thérèse of Lisieux: Her Last Conversations*). She even warned the sisters of her community not to leave anything poisonous nearby.

Even when we do all that we can to become whole again, illness forces us to face vulnerability. A young mother whose one-year-old son quickly recovered from a potentially lethal infection confessed, "He's fine, but now I have to recover from the whole frightening experience." She sharply realized her child's and her own vulnerability. One of the biggest losses from illness is the sense of being invincible.

Suffering and grief do not guarantee wisdom and compassion, but they may teach us empathy with our brothers and sisters and dependence on God's love and mercy.
Francis of Assisi, Teresa of Ávila, and Ignatius of Loyola
each turned their life around after long, serious illnesses.
Their illnesses made them see what was most essential in
life: love of their neighbor and of God. Ignatius, who
spent months recovering from injuries sustained when a
cannonball shattered his legs, remarked, "In these
afflictions...I can feel no sadness or pain, because I realize that a servant of God, through an illness, turns out to
be something of a doctor for the direction and ordering
of his life to God's glory and service" (William J. Young,
ed. and trans., *Letters of Saint Ignatius of Loyola*). As
with any loss, the outcome of our loss of health depends
on how we grieve over and make sense of the losses involved in our own life.

Reflection Exercises

♦ After breathing deeply and relaxing, become mindful
of the presence of God, who is full of love and caring for
you. Allow yourself to have a sense of God's wish to
heal and support you. Bring to mind whatever ailments,
weakness, or distress you may be experiencing. Become
aware of any pain or problems within your body. Simply hold whatever you are suffering in awareness before
God.

♦ As you consider the ailments or illnesses with which
you are burdened, begin to examine what they have asked

you to let go of—feelings of well-being? certain activities? the image you had of yourself? a sense of invulnerability? roles or jobs that you can no longer do? Are there any other losses you can identify? Attend to and release any of the feelings that emerge during your reflection.

◆ In your journal, write a dialogue with the one illness or condition from which you suffer most. Ask the illness what it is teaching you, how you can befriend it, how you can heal it, if possible. Invite Jesus into the conversation. Talk with him about the illness.

◆ Set a crucifix before you or hold it in your hand and begin to think about the losses Jesus may have experienced during his life, suffering, and death. List them and ponder how many may be like your own.

◆ What changes in your attitudes and behavior has illness or suffering asked of you? Do any of these changes enable you to live more healthfully and compassionately? Are you willing to make any adaptations that will help you manage your condition, or do you tend to resist those changes? Consider what changes are being asked of you and what feelings come with these changes. How might the illness or suffering be the vehicle for new life for you? How might it invite you to closer union with God?

◆ Think about what your illness may be teaching you. Ask God for help in seeing the lessons and opportunities you may not see.

◆ During her long struggle with tuberculosis, Elizabeth Ann Seton, the founder of the Sisters of Charity, a widowed mother of five children, and the first American to be declared a saint, confided, "Sickness does not frighten the secret peace of mind which is founded on a confidence in the divine goodness, and if death succeeds it, I must put a mother's hopes and fears in His hands Who has promised most to the widow and the fatherless" (Joseph I. Dirvin, *Mrs. Seton: Foundress of the American Sisters of Charity*).

◆ Ponder Elizabeth Seton's words and what they have to tell you about coping with your own illness and grief.

◆ Pray with God's Word. Apply it to your own situation, and let it speak to you.

God's Word

> *When my heart had been growing sour*
> *and I was pained in my innermost parts,*
> *I had been foolish and misunderstood;*
> . . . .
> *Nevertheless, I waited in your presence;*
> *you grasped my right hand.*
> *Now guide me with your counsel*
> *and receive me into glory at last.*
>
> —*Psalm 73:21–24*, Psalms Anew

The Spirit too comes to help us in our weakness....
We are well aware that God works with those who
love [God], those who have been called in accor-
dance with [God's] purpose, and turns everything
to their good.

—*Romans 8:26–28,* NJB

Closing prayer: God of healing, God of hope, heal me as you will and give me hope. You meet me in all my weaknesses and broken places. Help me to know your wholeness and power there. May my helplessness challenge me to find strength and healing in you.

REFLECTION 14

Home

"I don't feel like there's anyplace that's home anymore...."

Opening prayer: Living God, you have created the whole world as my home. Help me to find you here. Send your grace so that I may grieve over the loss of what home had been, let go of it, and know that I am never without a home in your love.

Story

Only as the children got together a month after the funeral, to pack up their mother's furniture and belongings, did it begin to sink in that their home had, in a way, died too. All four of them had their own homes and families but, somehow, closing up their childhood home added to their pain and sadness.

They had all grown up in the house where their mother had died, and every corner of it held memories. In the living room hung pictures of their German immigrant

104

grandparents, stoic expressions on faces that the children knew often laughed and warmed with tenderness. In their parents' bedroom stood the scarred oak rocking chair in which their mother had sung them to sleep. Up in the attic they uncovered a battle sword that their father had taken off of a dead Japanese officer in Okinawa. They remembered all their futile attempts as children to get their dad to tell stories of the war. He would shake his head somberly and simply say no.

Even after each child married, they lived nearby and visited frequently. Whenever any of them talked about "going home" for the holidays or special occasions, there was never any confusion about where they meant. Home was here—their first home, their place of connection and grounding.

Even the spouses seemed at home here. And their own children had explored the special places of the old house. Even now as they packed away their memories and decided the fate of their parents' possessions, the shouts and laughter of their children playing outside blew in through the open windows. The big old house and the surrounding land invited play.

Their mother's death had been expected. After three awful years of battling cancer, she welcomed death. During the last months, her pain had grown so intense that her children welcomed her death too. When it finally came, relief mixed with their grief. They missed their mother—especially here. Her presence permeated the house. When the children talked about their feelings, they discovered that each of them kept expecting to see their mother appear.

Closing the family home was proving harder than

predicted. Robert voiced what they were all thinking. "This feels awful. I can't believe we won't be coming back here. It's like the end not only of Mom but of everything else too. Why do we have to give this place up? I feel like I'm being turned loose in the world with no place to go. I don't feel like there's anyplace that's really home anymore." Tears edged out of Robert's eyes, and soon they were all weeping.

"It feels like we're saying good-bye to Mom all over again."

"Remember when we used to sit on the front porch in the evening, and Dad would tell us scary stories? And what about the time Mary Ann tried to bake a blackberry pie and dropped it as it came out of the oven! After she stopped crying, we sat down and ate it up off the floor!" Jerry remembered.

Memory followed memory. They laughed, cried, and reminisced. With the memories came sadness and pain, warmth and love, and even some old antipathies. They also wondered about the future. "I'm scared we're going to lose track of one another if we don't have this place to come back to," Mary Ann mused.

Finally, as the sun began to sink and their children started wandering into the house, they seemed to sigh in unison. Nodding to one another, they silently continued sorting through and putting away the remnants of home.

Commentary

We all have an inner longing to be "at home," to be in the right place. If our childhood was relatively happy, we often locate such a feeling in our family home. If our childhood held abuse, pain, or lovelessness, our homes may carry difficult and painful memories. We perhaps never had a true home.

Ideally home is a place of safety and nurturance. It is where we belong. Home helps to tell us who we are. Indeed, the symbolic value of home far surpasses the actual physical building. Most of the time the value of home has little to do with its physical form. When home is connected to images of parents who loved us, it stands for security in this world. We knew what to expect there and what was expected of us. Home builds an image into our heart that accompanies us on life's journeys. It provides a psychic home base amid the vagaries of the world.

Even when we may have been hurt in our homes by those from whom we expected care, we seem to carry an image of what we wished might have been. The house we grew up in still stands in our memory and shapes us. We may spend our life searching for an ideal home that never existed. We may spend enormous emotional energy making sense out of our childhood home. Even the loss of an abusive home leaves a gap in our life and calls forth our grief.

Multiple losses cluster around the loss of home. For an elderly or widowed spouse, or someone who can no longer manage a home, moving into an apartment, in with a child, or to a nursing home means letting go of cherished, comforting possessions accumulated over a lifetime. Tears streamed down the cheeks of one nursing home resident when she told me, "The hardest thing for me to leave behind was my dog. Beauty was always with me. She was a wonderful companion, and I miss her so!"

When a home goes up in flames, washes away in a flood, or is scattered in a tornado, the residents are left bewildered and insecure. Suddenly the whole world becomes a threat. Losing the tangible reminders of past events often feels like losing one's history, one's sense of self. We may try to deny our grief, but attempting to avoid the pain by minimizing our loss delays our letting go and moving on. As with all other losses, we begin our grieving by identifying the losses. Because our home is so interwoven with our sense of self, many emotions will arise as we attempt to let it go. Some of our emotions might surprise us and, if we attend to them, we may discover a loss we had not realized was so important. Expressing and sharing our feelings, especially with family members, may help us make decisions about how to adjust to and deal with the loss of our home.

Reflection Exercises

♦ Take some deep breaths and relax, becoming as comfortable as possible. Call to mind the places you've called home throughout your life. Linger over those homes that were in some way remarkable to you—either for good or ill. Note the ones that become foremost in your mind, especially the one or two that had the greatest impact on you. Choose the home you miss the most and think about what was helpful and positive there. Write about this home in your journal; describe its special places, its smells, its poignant memories. Be aware of your feelings, and let them be.

♦ If your home was negative or harmful for you, call that to mind now. Though painful, try to be specific about just what was lost. Identify the hurts and the aspects of home that were not there for you. As you recall or write, honor your feelings and attend to them.

If you are ready to let go of this home and all it represents, present it to God, praying: "I give you the ... (for instance, abuse or coldness) that I felt in my home, and ask you to let me feel your great love for me. May I make my home in you, merciful God, my father and mother." Accompanying this prayer with some ritual may help in the letting go.

♦ Picture the childhood home that is most important to you (presuming that you may have had more than one). In your journal, spontaneously list key events that happened there. Describe the appearance of your parent(s) and your sibling(s) as you remember them from your childhood. What image or metaphor captures what "home" was like for you while you were growing up? You may try imaging your experience of home by using watercolors, crayons, colored pencils, or felt markers to paint or draw a mandala, a circular graphic representation of your image of, in this case, home, using colors, symbols, or figures. Drawing the mandala may evoke many feelings and realizations; explaining the mandala may stir even more insights.

In a dialogue with the Holy Spirit, write about how your experience of home, whatever it may have been, has affected your life. Discuss any aspects of losing your home that you still need to grieve about. Share your feelings. The Holy Spirit may pose questions, support, and affirm you.

◆ Meditate on the following poem written by Teresa of
Ávila:

> *Let nothing trouble you,*
> *Let nothing scare you,*
> *All is fleeting,*
> *God alone is unchanging.*
> *Patience*
> *Everything obtains.*
> *Who possesses God*
> *Nothing wants.*
> *God alone suffices.*
>
> —*Kavanaugh,* Collected Works
> of St. Teresa of Ávila

◆ Then ponder these questions:

   ❖ Do I believe that God makes a home within
me?

   ❖ What kind of a home within me do I provide
for God?

   ❖ Am I at home with myself?

   ❖ Am I at home in the world? Have I made a home
for my spirit as well as my body?

◆ Ponder God's Word. Slowly repeat a phrase that you
find most challenging or affirming; let its implications
for you become clear.

God's Word

One thing have I asked of you, Yahweh,
this I seek:
to dwell in your house
all the days of my life.

—*Psalm 27:4*, Psalms Anew

Do not let your hearts be troubled. Believe in God,
believe also in me. In [God's] house there are many
dwelling places....I go to prepare a place for you.

—*John 14:1–2*, NRSV

[God] will give you another Advocate, to be with
you forever....[The Spirit] abides with you, and...in
you. I will not leave you orphaned.

—*John 16–18*, NRSV

Closing prayer: Welcoming God, you are the home I am searching for. Help me to be grateful for whatever gifts were in my home. Lead me through my grieving for the goodness of my home or for the home I wish I had. May I let go of my grief and build a home with you inside me, a place of warmth and comfort, to guide and nurture me.

Independence

"I don't have anything to say about anything anymore...."

Opening prayer: God of life and completion, open my eyes to see how the gradual loss of my independence can be a source of movement and growth into greater dependence on you. Be with me in my journey.

Story

Jack was his own man from the time he was eighteen years old. He knew he could rely on himself. He married, and he and his wife, Margaret, had four boys. Jack supported his sons all through college, into jobs and lives of their own. Even when his own job disappeared as the company he worked for collapsed, he had worked odd jobs until he found a better position. He came to believe that he could handle whatever life dished out. He managed even through the devastation of his dear Margaret's death.

Now Jack knew that things were slipping out of his hands. At eighty-six, he had seen the loss of control coming in little ways, but he would not admit it, even to himself. Despite new glasses, he could hardly read. When he drove, street signs looked fuzzy and indecipherable. He would probably not pass the test for a new license. One day, he had forgotten a pot of soup cooking on the stove. The smell of the charred pan was the only thing that saved him from fire. The doctor kept telling him that he was heading for trouble if he did not eat better. Then a fall left a lingering pain in his hip.

His sons kept hedging around the idea of a nursing home. Jack adamantly resisted. "I'd rather die than go live in a place like that. I can handle this. If I can just have a little more time and try a little harder, everything will work out. It always has."

Commentary

Independence—our ability to live life as we choose, under our own steam—is one of our most prized possessions. Independence lets us feel competent and self-directed. We relish being in control of our own life and resist any loss of independence. However, acknowledging our dependence and giving up some of the control of our life is frequently part of the aging process. Our senses, our muscles, and our mind begin to lose their facility, no matter how much attention and effort we put into their maintenance.

Our first job in coming to terms with our gradually diminishing independence is to acknowledge the ways we have lost control. Even calling these losses to mind

may be difficult because we try so hard to convince ourself and others that we can handle our life. While the
positive approach may help us continue fending for ourself to some degree, acknowledging the losses may help
us cope more realistically.

Retiring or losing a job—in a society that values and
defines us by what we "do"—may make us feel useless
and of little value. Illnesses, both acute and chronic, may
leave us less able to care for ourselves. Each illness brings
along a whole set of attached losses. We may not be able
to shop, visit, or attend church. We may become dependent on visiting nurses for care, and on family members
and friends for transportation and company. Accidents
and injuries may limit us to bed or a wheelchair at any
age. Being dependent on glasses, hearing aids, or canes
can distress us, even if we are in our teens.

Each curtailment of our independence reminds us of
how little we really do control. Certainly each of us has
a unique story to tell about our accumulating loss of
independence. To grieve and let go, we need to identify
our losses of independence, noting each one in particular. Without acknowledging each loss, the general feeling of loss can permeate our life. Soon we can feel like
we are losing all direction of our own affairs, even if we
are far from doing so.

Sensing little control in our own life can bring on feelings of helplessness and hopelessness, followed often by
anger or despair. We may become furious with those who
we believe are trying to regulate our life or who seem to
be keeping us from doing things for ourselves. God may
be the object of our anger. A cry I have heard is, "I pray
and pray and have always tried to be a good person,

why is God doing this to me? I feel like I'm being punished!" These feelings may hang on when we refuse to move through our grieving.

Adjusting to loss of independence in a hopeful way also involves changing some of our lifestyle patterns. First, we need to examine what physical behaviors we are holding onto that may be dangerous. For example, climbing on the roof to clean leaves out of the downspouts may have to be set aside. If our eyesight and reflexes do not allow us to drive safely, we have to let go of driving, out of charity to ourselves and to other people. No matter how logical such changes may be, making them is not easy, and we will feel the pain of loss.

On the other hand, a realistic look at our situation may show us ways to increase our independence. Marlene resisted moving out of her home for years, even after she had to stop driving. She became a virtual prisoner in her home, and had to depend on one of her nieces to take her on errands. When she moved into an apartment complex for older people, she was able to be out and about, taking the shuttle to the malls and riding with new friends to bingo games and polka dances. Letting go of her previous independence had actually permitted new freedom.

Acknowledging the loss of our independence, expressing our feelings about it, and deciding to let go will never be easy, but this grieving process can be an opening to new life. A choice for change may include renewed involvement with friends, with family members, with other people in need, and with God. When we cease our busyness and assess the many wonders of life, we may decide to spend more time with our Creator and Sustainer. We always have choices in our inner life—our thoughts, spirits, and attitudes. No one can control our wonder at the sunrise, our glee over a good joke—the small daily miracles. Living is not over, even if it is different.

Reflection Exercises

◆ Relax, breathe deeply, and be comfortable. Begin to think through the past few years up to the present. Note the ways you feel loss of some control and independence. List them in your journal. You may be helped by answering questions like these:

❖ How is my body (sight, hearing, strength) not able to keep up with what I've done in the past or the things I would like to do now?

❖ When do I need to ask for help and resent it?

❖ When do I get exasperated with myself because I can't do what I think I should be able to do?

❖ What ailments or failings keep me attached to seeking treatment or being dependent on others for my care?

❖ Do I forget, and then get impatient with myself for poor memory?

❖ In what situations do I feel incompetent because I don't understand—or have never learned— some new ways of doing things?

❖ How angry do I get with others who try to control me, tell me what to do, boss me around? When does that happen?

❖ How upset am I with myself for not being like I used to be?

◆ After you have reviewed your feelings of helplessness and lack of control, meditate on how these losses have affected you in all manner of ways. Attend to your feelings. If tears flow, know that they help to wash away the pain of the loss. If anger erupts, accept it as showing how much you enjoyed your independence and how hard it is to let it go.

If you find dialogue with Jesus or a wisdom figure from your past helpful, write a dialogue with him or her about your feelings. Here are some questions that might spur your discussion:

❖ Am I feeling abandoned by God and angry because I'm not the able-bodied, capable person I was in my younger days? Do I feel like God is punishing me for something?

❖ Do I rebel against natural processes in life? Am I angry about my normal life passages? Do I perhaps think I shouldn't have to go through these losses?

❖ If I feel despairing or depressed, where are these feelings coming from?

❖ Is fear of dying behind some of my anger?

◆ Consider what changes in your behavior may be helpful in coping with your loss of control or independence. What about your attitude might have to be changed? Write a plan of living for yourself—a practical plan to live lovingly, hopefully, and faithfully under your changed circumstances. Write specifics of that plan to do something you have avoided or to reach out to another person.

◆ Meditate on Ignatius of Loyola's famous prayer of surrender. Ask God how you can make it your own surrender to God's will and care:

> *Take, Lord, and receive all my liberty, my memory, my understanding, and my entire will, all that I have and possess. You have given all to me. To you, Lord, I return it. All is yours. Dispose of it wholly according to your will. Give me your love and your grace. That is enough for me.*
>
> —*Elisabeth Meier Tetlow*, Spiritual Exercises

◆ Pray with God's Word. Converse with God about how these words are Good News for you.

God's Word

> *Blessed be…God…who gives every possible encouragement; [who] supports us in every hardship, so that we are able to come to the support of others, in every hardship of theirs because of the encouragement that we ourselves receive from God. For just as the sufferings of Christ overflow into our lives; so too does the encouragement we receive through Christ.*
>
> —*2 Corinthians 1:3–6*, NJB

> *In the world you will have hardship, but be courageous: I [Jesus] have conquered the world.*
>
> —*John 16:33*, NJB

Closing prayer: Holy Friend, help me to experience my wholeness in you. Let me know that you are with me through all the losses in my life, supporting me in my need. Help me to accept support now as I have supported others in the past. I thank you for all the gifts of my life, even those I must now relinquish. Transform my distress at growing more dependent into the substance of new life and strength in you.

One's Own Life

"I feel like I'm losing everything...."

Opening prayer: God of life and death, you know what a hard time I have facing death and letting go of all the gifts of this world. Teach me how to face my dying. Be with me in my suffering and sadness, in the "valley of the shadow of death" with all its fear. Lead me to new life in your embrace.

Story

Jeanie stayed as active as she could: working, cooking, taking care of her family, crocheting colorful afghans, and tending her yard. She loved planting flowers in the spring, digging in the moist loam, and even mowing the lawn. But each activity took added effort now, and she sometimes found herself frozen by her musings.

Jeanie knew that she was going to die. Over two years ago, weakness in her legs and a persistent, hacking cough prompted a visit to her doctor. All she wanted was an antibiotic, but the doctor insisted on x-rays, blood work, and other tests. Her weakness and coughing were the beginning signs of lung cancer.

When she started chemotherapy, she proclaimed, "I'll beat this." The chemotherapy seemed to do its job. Even though her hair had fallen out—a hard loss—Jeanie's spirits lifted. Her appreciation of life deepened, and she shared her joy at being alive. Patients and staff at the clinic were delighted to see her come for her checkups with enthusiasm and humor.

After a brief period of optimism, the cancer returned, this time invading other places in her body. She felt life slipping away. In dread, she cried, "How could I not be here? My kids, what's going to happen? And the hardest thing is knowing I won't ever see my grandkids."

Thoughts of what she was going to lose sometimes crept into—and sometimes flooded—her awareness. Roses of all colors, lilacs, green expanses of rolling hills brought her to tears. Memories of her old dogs, the half-planted row of tomatoes, and her lost raccoon wandered in and out of her mind, along with thoughts of family, friends, people from work, and places she still wanted to visit. Pondering all these beautiful things brought her poignant sadness.

Jeanie's hope faltered, and sadness pervaded each waking moment. Looking into a mirror shocked her. Her figure, color, and strength were drained away. Even crocheting sapped her shrinking energy. Work was out of the question.

As the pain intensified, she would cry out. She felt helpless, unable to change the pain. "I can't concentrate on anything. Even reading's impossible." The cancer was inexorably stripping Jeanie of everything that she valued, even attacking her faith. To her sister, she confessed sadly, "I just don't understand why God doesn't hear me. I pray and pray and things only seem to get worse." Even so, she kept praying.

Toward the end, Jeanie somehow found her own peace. Through all the suffering, pain, doubt, and sadness, she faced the final challenge that this life presented to her. Her last words testified to her acceptance of the ultimate loss of this world, and her transition to the next. She whispered, "I hope I can do this well!"

Commentary

The process of our dying can strip us of any illusions that we have of invulnerability and control. The process is also one of grieving. Nevertheless, if we approach our dying consciously, we have the opportunity to choose life and growth. Thea Bowman, a well-known Franciscan sister whose life and ministry were within the black Catholic community, lived with cancer for six years before she died in 1991. When asked about how she managed, Thea said, "I want to choose life, I want to keep going, I want to live fully until I die." And she did. Sister Thea maintained an extensive schedule of speaking engagements and workshop presentations even when she had to use a wheelchair and was sick from chemotherapy.

Certainly each individual comes to death at the end of a unique and personal journey. If we have a history of denying our difficulties, accepting the inevitability of our own death may prove very hard. As in all instances of loss, to die well means to get past that denial and to release our emotions. Often these movements walk hand in hand. Our manner of acknowledging death and letting go will echo the ways we have dealt uniquely with other losses.

Emotions may ravage us. Our sense of helplessness may trigger a rage at our caregivers, family, friends, and God. When our illness has been brought on by unhealthy choices of our own, guilt may whip us. And, of course, sadness permeates our waking hours, especially as the scope of our loss comes more completely into focus.

Dying people sometimes try to stay strong and in control for the duration of their last days. But allowing our emotions to flow, talking about our feelings, and accepting support from listeners all help us to make our way through the grief. Sister Thea offered this advice about letting go of our feelings:

My people used to say—and still say—sometimes you have to moan....I've found that moaning is therapeutic. It's a way of centering, the way you do in centering prayer. You concentrate your internal energies and your powers in prayer or wordless outcry to God....

I moan sometimes, I sing sometimes....When I have pain, I find it goes away when I hum or sing.

Talk about what you're thinking and what you're feeling. Talk about what you need and what you want. Talk about what you see, and talk about your experiences. Invite people to share a prayer with you. Generally, let people know where you are. Often folks will stand around waiting and

*wanting to help. Only you, as the sick person, can
tell them what they can do.*

—Taylor, "Lord, Let Me Live Till I Die," Praying

Even if we are angry with God, holding in the anger
does little good. Besides, God knows what is in our heart
anyway. As in human relationships, stifling what we feel
can strain the connections. If we tell God what we feel,
God has a chance to join in the conversation.

As we acknowledge our dying and let our emotions
flow, we can also make some decisions about our departure from this world. Perhaps we need to unclutter our
lives. Maybe, as one client did, we need to sort out our
treasures and unclutter our minds of worries and regrets.
Rita remarked peacefully, "Letting go of so many things
inside me and outside me gave me a much freer sense of
myself and even helped me feel better physically."

Simplifying our life can then help us focus on the essentials and the beauty of life—loving relationships and
the little wonders. A physician friend who was dying
told me, "I can sit and look at the sky for hours, it's just
so beautiful. And I don't see grass anymore. I see *blades*
of grass."

Addressing and resolving old conflicts can add to the
peace of our passing too. Unfinished business can be a
source of ongoing distress for a dying person, as well as
for the bereaved people left behind. And of course some
of the unfinished business may literally be business. Tragi-
cally, too often people who deny that they are dying do
not put their will, finances, and obligations in order while
they can. When they die, their family or friends are left
to untangle the mess.

We have choices about our dying. Though we may not know the day or hour, we can prepare for it by grieving all the little deaths and other losses well. When the final loss faces us we can "do it well."

Reflection Exercises

◆ After you have settled yourself, relax and breathe deeply and slowly. Remind yourself that you are held in God's hands. When you feel ready, call to mind any losses you are experiencing, or will experience, in your dying. Which of these losses causes you the most distress? As you list the losses, which stir the most feeling?

◆ What changes in your relationships, lifestyle, work, and spirituality would eliminate regrets at the time of your death? Is there any uncluttering of your life that you could do right now to allow yourself greater freedom to appreciate life? Create an image in your mind of what feels cluttered in your life, and then let your mind begin to eliminate the clutter. How does this feel? Decide on at least one thing to let go of now. Offer this thing to God, saying: "I release this ... from my life. I give it to you, Living God, as a sign of detaching myself from what is unnecessary, superfluous. Teach me to love life and to embrace the essentials."

◆ Is there any unfinished business with another person—antipathies, unexpressed love—that could be finished now so that life can be more full for both of you? Ponder this question, and then act on any resolution that you come to.

♦ If fear and anxiety about death settle in you, pray this prayer or one of your own: "O God, see my fear and worry when I ponder my own death. Be with me now and calm my heart. I release to you all of my distress, especially my fear about .... Help me to know in my whole being that you will ask nothing of me without being right there with me, sharing in my experience. Grant me your great peace."

Or pray with Jesus: "Into your hands, loving God, I commend my spirit." If it helps you release your feelings, moan, hum, or sing.

♦ Meditate on this advice, given by Sister Thea, about coming close to God as we die. Ask yourself what this tells you about your own death:

> I used to feel I could depend upon myself. I used to feel that I could make you a promise and that I could keep a promise. I could tell you that I would be coming to Chicago on a certain date, and I would board a plane and be there....
>
> I used to say, "It's all in God's hands." But only now do I really know what those words mean because I've experienced them.
>
> I'm so much more grateful than I used to be. I woke up this morning and I could move my legs—I say, "Thank you, God." I woke up this morning and the pain was less than it was a day or two ago—I say, "Thank you, God."

I don't despair because I believe God leads me and guides me, and I believe that I can reach out for God's hand. I have received such love and so many gifts. That's a part of what I hope at this time in my life to be able to share. I want to say to people just keep on keeping on.

—Tuohy, "Sister Thea Bowman:
On the Road to Glory"

♦ Sing a favorite hymn that celebrates your life and the promise of the Resurrection or that declares your deep faith in God's abundant mercy—for example, any version of the Twenty-Third Psalm, "Amazing Grace," or "How Can I Keep From Singing?"

God's Word

Then I heard a voice from heaven say to me, "Write down: Blessed are those who die in the Lord! Blessed indeed, the Spirit says; now they can rest for ever after their work, since their good deeds go with them."

—Revelations 14:13, NJB

We want you to be quite certain...about those who have fallen asleep, to make sure that you do not grieve for them, as others do who have no hope. We believe that Jesus died and rose again, and that in the same way God will bring [back] those who have fallen asleep in Jesus.

—1 Thessalonians 4:13–14, NJB

Closing prayer: Eternal, merciful God, I am in your hands in my living and my dying. May I always be ready to let go of this life. Let me love, hope, and be faithful now so that in my dying I may go without regret into the new life you have prepared for me. Amen. Alleluia.

Acknowledgments

The scriptural citations noted as NJB are from *The New Jerusalem Bible*. Copyright © 1985 by Darton, Longman & Todd, Ltd. and Doubleday, a division of Bantam, Doubleday, Dell Publishing Inc. Reprinted by permission.

The scriptural citations noted as NRSV are from the *New Revised Standard Version of the Bible*. Copyright © 1989 by the Division of Christian Education of the National Council of the Churches of Christ in the United States of America. All rights reserved.

The psalms on pages 32, 56, 70–71, 78, 102, and 111 are from *Psalms Anew: In Inclusive Language,* compiled by Nancy Schreck and Maureen Leach (Winona, Minn.: Saint Mary's Press, 1986), copyright © 1986 by Saint Mary's Press. All rights reserved.

All other scriptural material in this book is freely adapted and is not to be understood or used as an official translation of the Bible.

The excerpt on page xvi is from Mike Wallace's Foreword to *Sister Thea Bowman: Shooting Star* edited by Celestine Cepress (Winona, Minn.: Saint Mary's Press, 1993), page 9. Copyright © 1993 by Saint Mary's Press. All rights reserved.

The excerpts on pages xvi and 126–129 from Patrice J. Tuohy's interview with Thea Bowman are from "Sister Thea Bowman: On the Road to Glory," *U.S. Catholic* (June 1990): 21–26. Reprinted with permission from *U.S. Catholic* magazine, published by Claretian Publications, 205 W. Monroe Street, Chicago, IL 60606.

The excerpt on page 99 is from *St. Thérèse of Lisieux: Her Last Conversations*, translated by John Clarke, O.C.D. Copyright © 1977 by Washington Province of Discalced Carmelites, Inc., ICS Publications, 2131 Lincoln Road, N.E., Washington, DC 20002. Reprinted with permission.

The excerpt on page 100 is from *Letters of Saint Ignatius of Loyola*, edited and translated by William J. Young (Chicago: Loyola University Press, 1959), page 10. Copyright © 1959 by The Institute of Jesuit Sources.

The excerpt on page 102 is from *Mrs. Seton: Foundress of the American Sisters of Charity* by Joseph I. Dirvin (New York: Farrar, Straus and Giroux, 1962), page 218. Copyright © 1962 by Farrar, Straus and Giroux.

The excerpt on page 110 is from *The Collected Works of St. Teresa of Ávila*, Volume Three, translated by Kieran Kavanaugh and Otilio Rodriguez. Copyright © 1985 by the Washington Province of Discalced Carmelites, ICS Publications, 2131 Lincoln Road, N.E., Washington, DC 20002. Reprinted with permission.

The excerpt on page 118 is from *The Spiritual Exercises of Saint Ignarius Loyola,* translated by Elisabeth Meier Tetlow (Lanham, Md.: University Press of America, 1987), page 79. Copyright © 1987 by the College Theology Society, University Press of America. Reprinted with permission.

The excerpt on pages 123–124 from Fabvienen Taylor's interview with Thea Bowman is from "Lord, Let Me Live Till I Die," *Praying* (Nov–Dec 1989): 19–22. Reprinted with permission of *Praying* magazine.